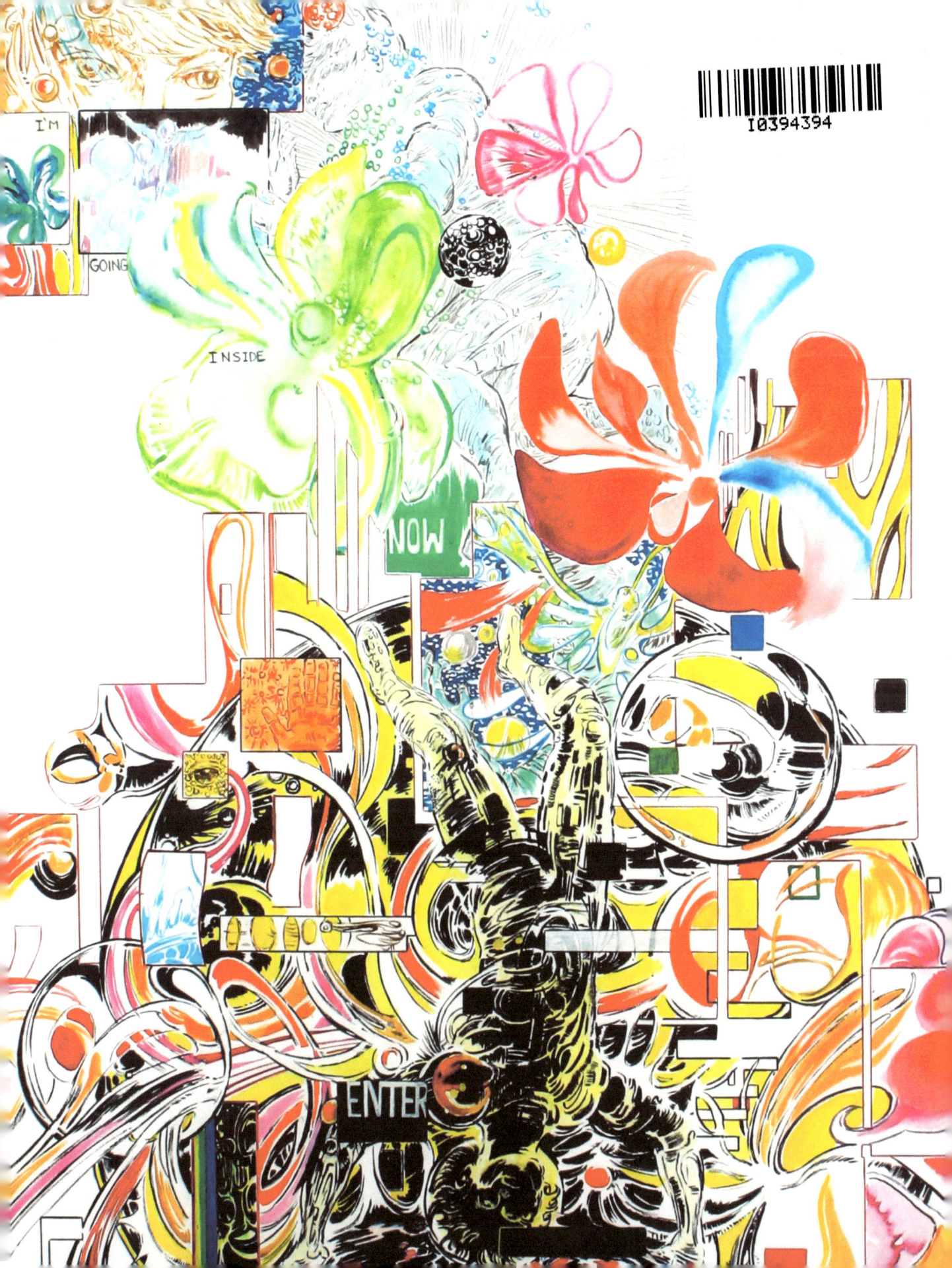

I0394394

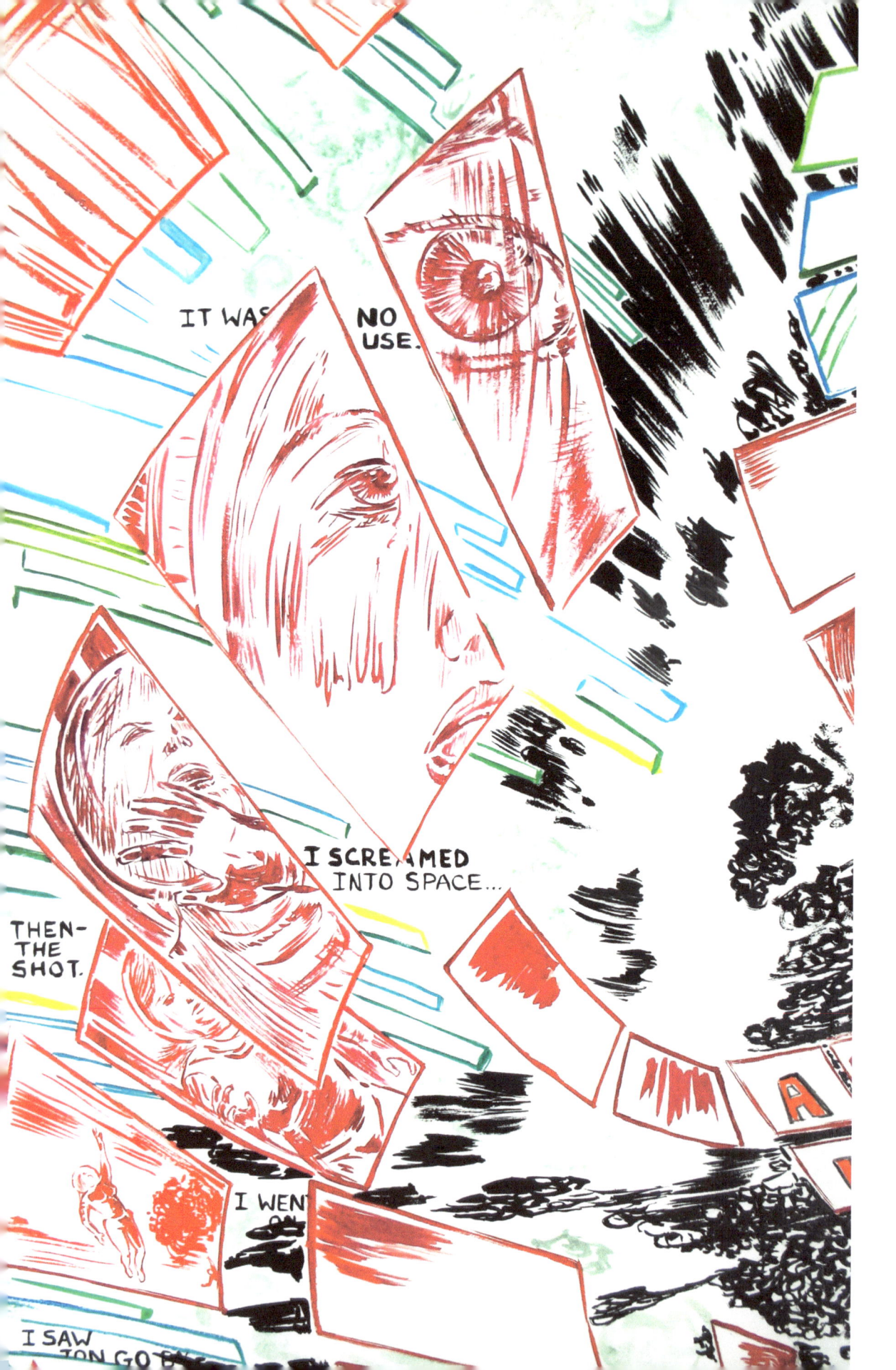

NEW DRAWING
VICTORY HALL PRESS

New Drawing

April 2011

Copyright ©2011 Victory Hall Press

website: www.victoryhall.org

www.universechild.net

contact: victoryhall1@msn.com

Victory Hall Press

PO Box 324

Jersey City, NJ

07324-0324

ISBN-13:

978-0615448206 (Victory Hall Press)

ISBN-10:

0615448208

Exhibition:

James Pustorino:*Universechild*

March 3 - April 30, 2011

CHAMBERS @916, Portland, Oregon

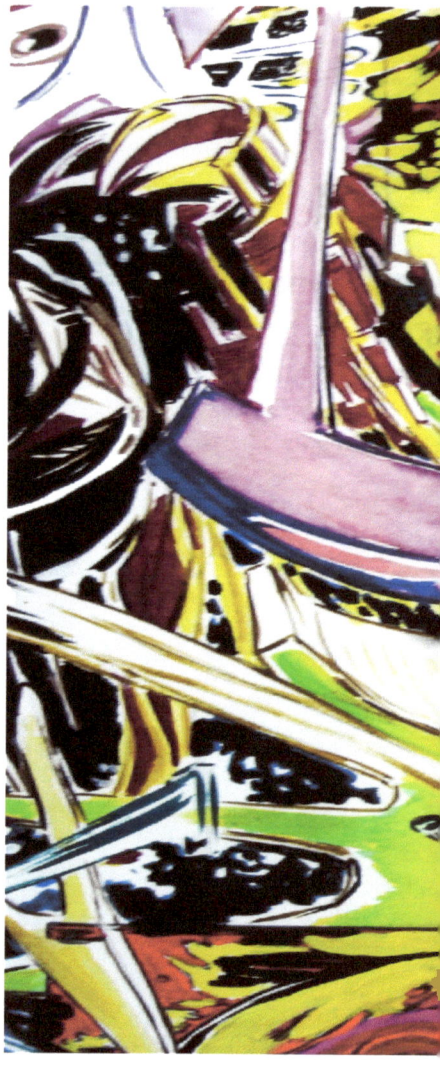

This program is made possible in part by funds from the New Jersey State Council on the Arts/Department of State, a partner agency of the National Endowment for the Arts, administered by the Hudson County office of Cultural and Heritage affairs, Thomas A. Degise, county executive, and the board of chosen freeholders.

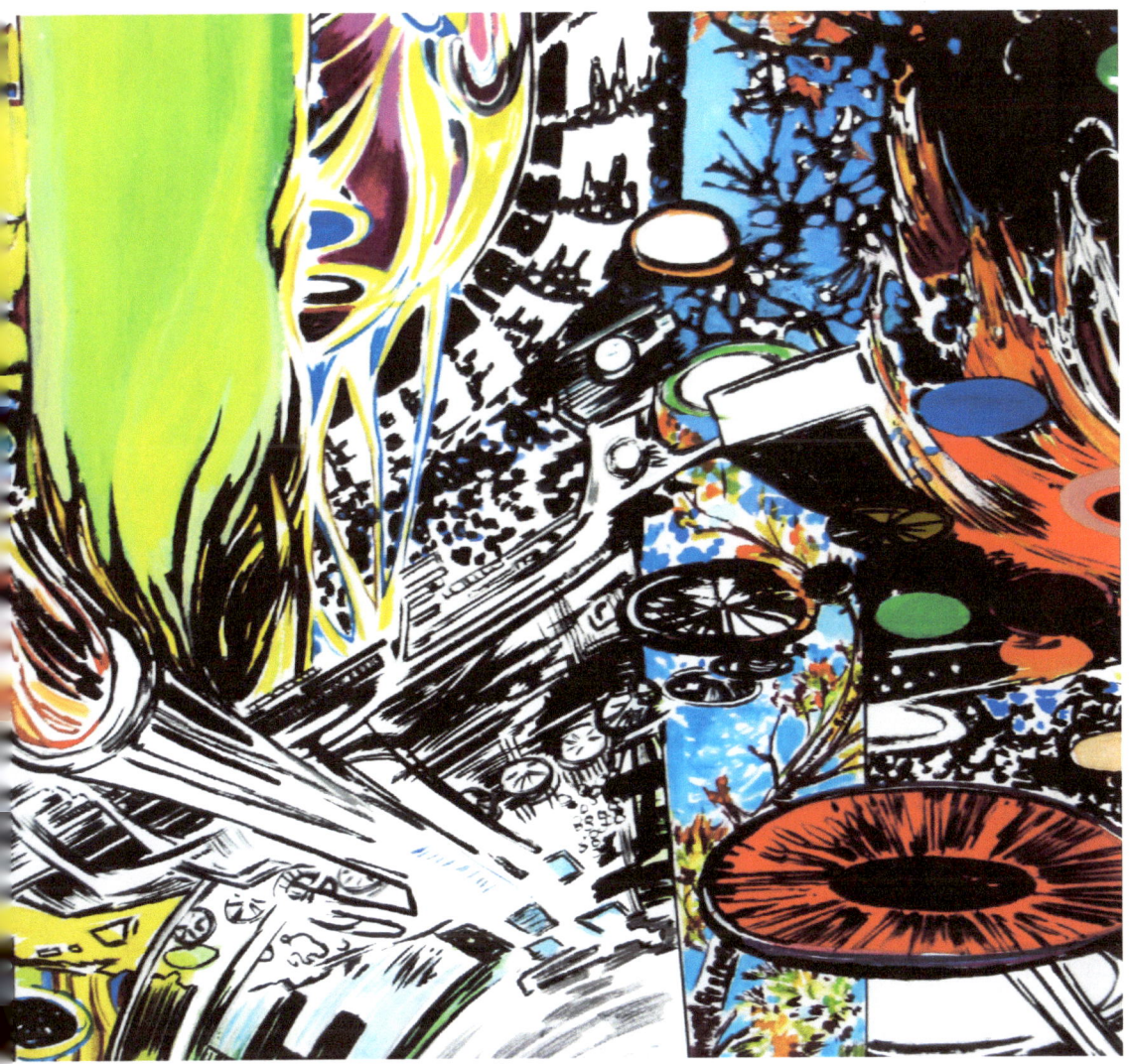

james pustorino
UNIVERSECHILD

for Jim Campbell

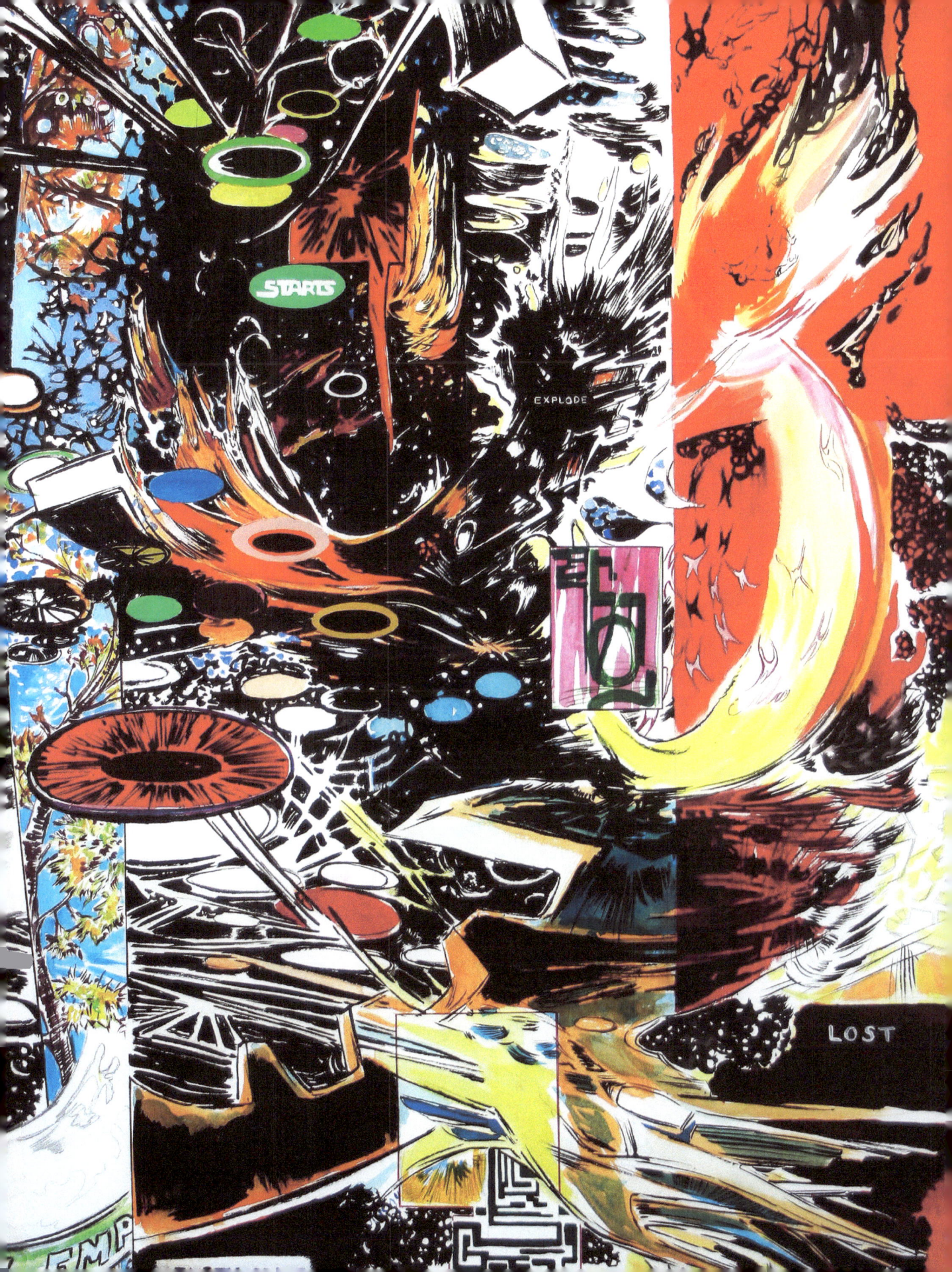

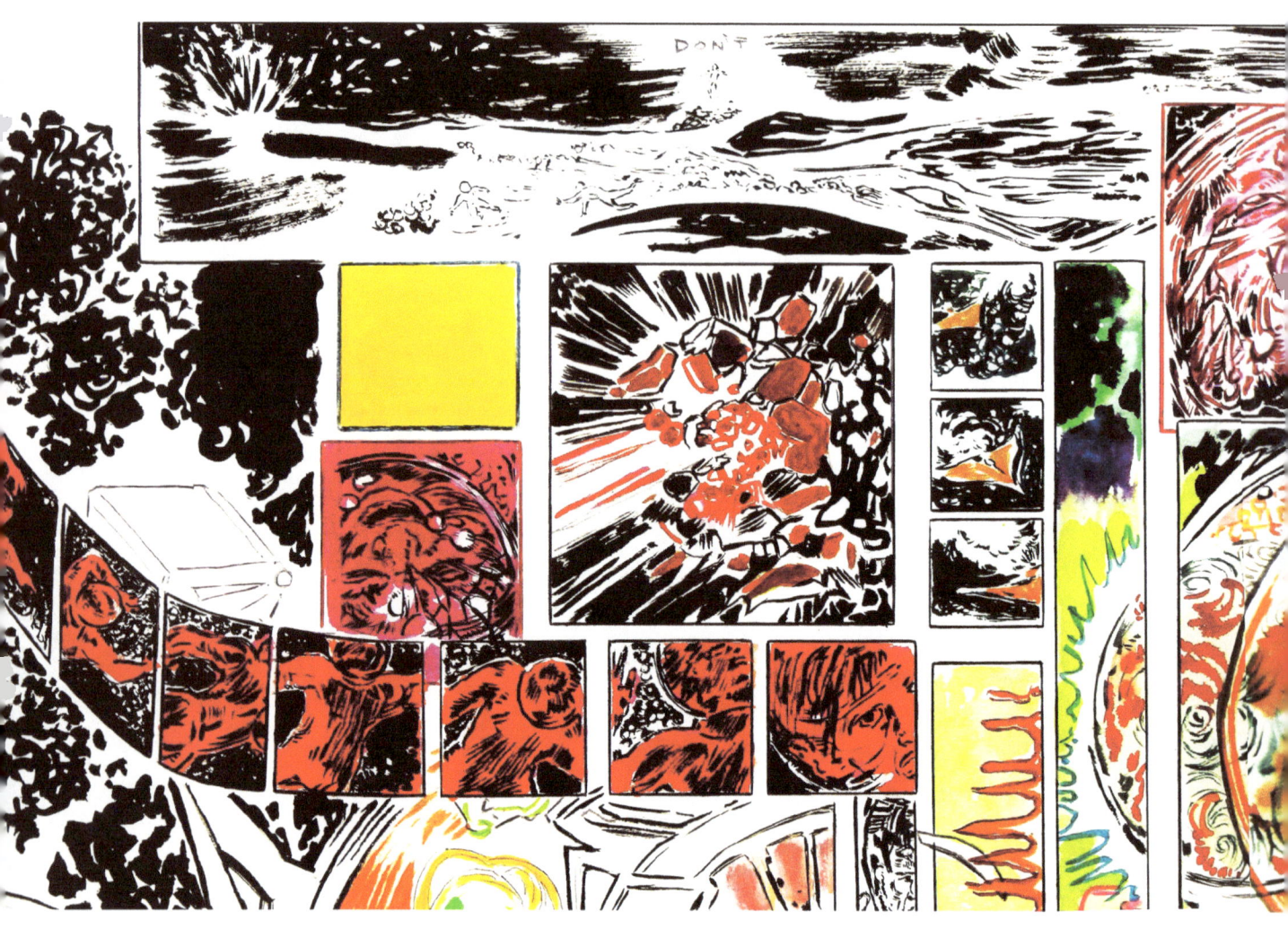

NEW DRAWING
VICTORY HALL PRESS

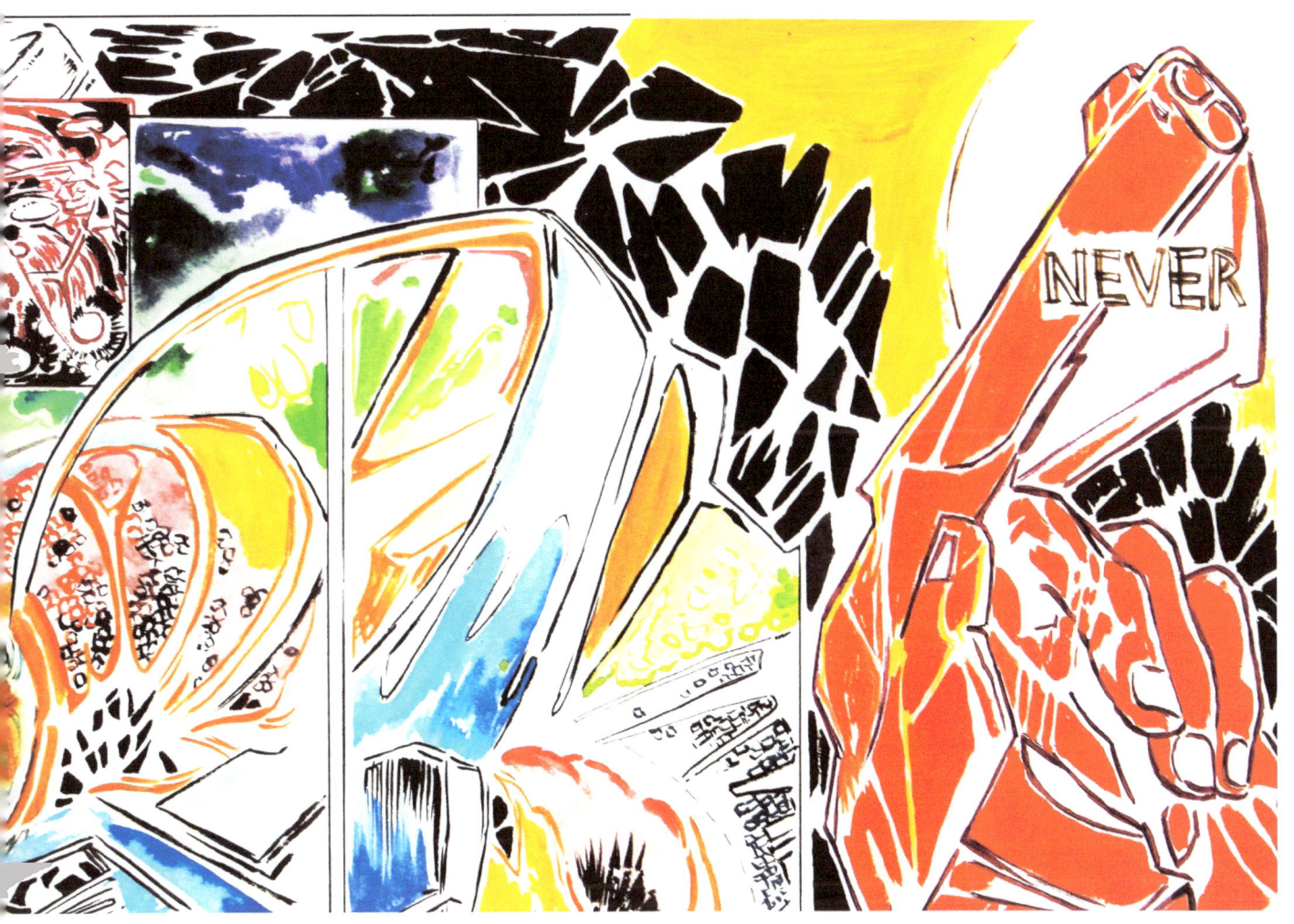

james pustorino

UNIVERSECHILD

Artist's Note on the Making of Universechild

The Universechild project is the result of a life-long fascination with the comic strip and comic book as a narrative form, paired with an ambition to reach beyond the constraints of normal storytelling and create a set of work with few limits. It was started as an effort to create an inventive drawing language that was inclusive of elements from the content and imagery of popular culture. The working method, derived from that of the surrealists and abstract expressionists in the early/mid 1900s, is one in which the artist allows form and content to develop as one draws, accepting and wrestling with the imagery and compositions that grow there. Although I made a lot of other art during this period, the drawings developed over several years and the series was finally completed in early 2011.

The Universechild is something you look for. It's a bit in the spirit of William Blake's drawings for Dante's Divine Comedy: Paradisio to Inferno. The boy searches for himself; the mother searches for her son; the father is invisible, waiting to be searched for; and everyone is searching for the Universechild.

-James Pustorino

" James Pustorino synthesizes science fiction, comic books, Abstract Expressionism and psychedelic art, all in the service of approximating the profound mystery of existence. A mythic narrative about a being born into space, where he struggles to understand his surroundings and purpose. It's the sort of existential crisis everyone inevitably faces, but Pustorino translates that mental anguish into physical upheaval, as this particular being is born, like a star, in outer space, amid planets and darting rockets. "

- John Motley, *The Oregonian*

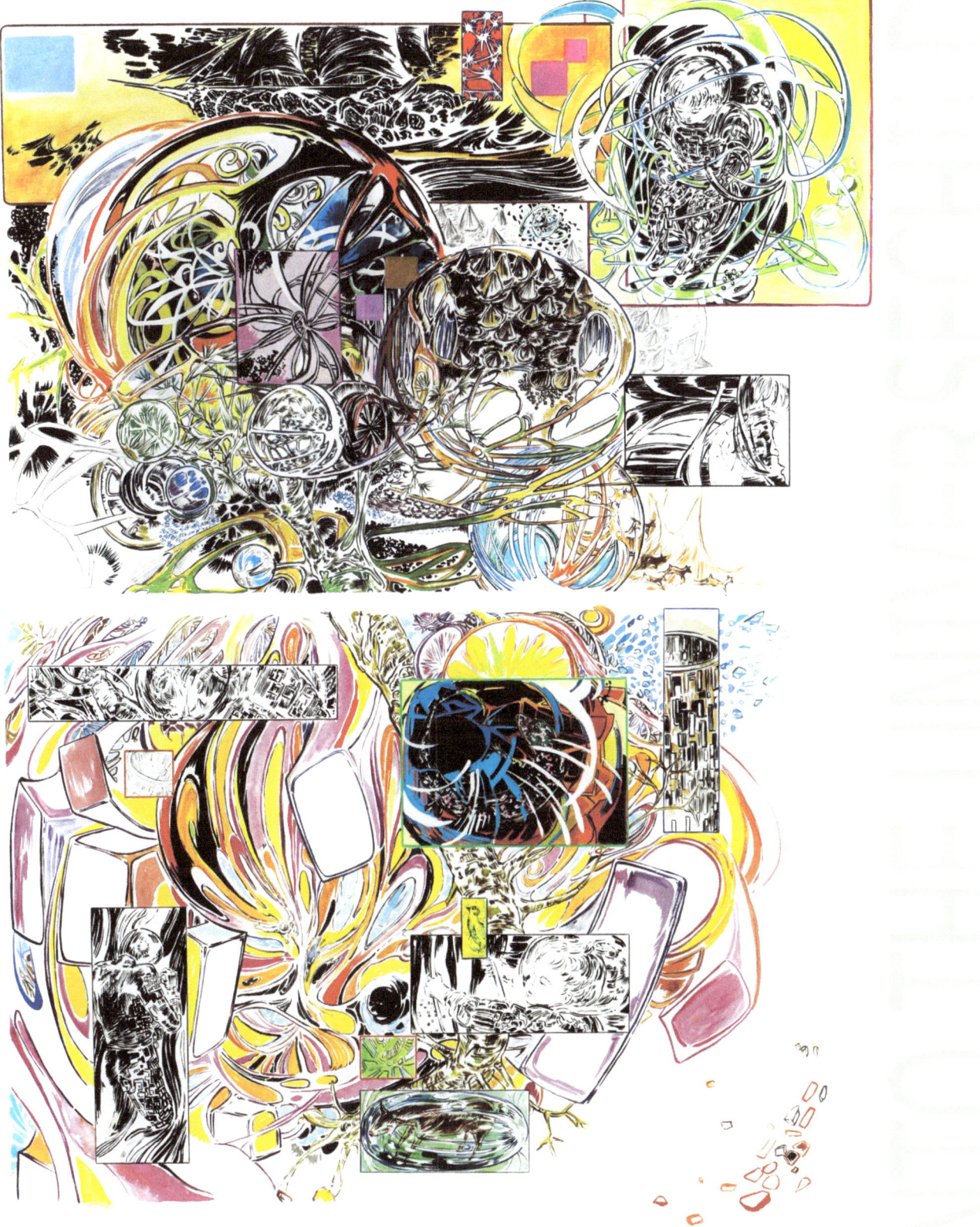

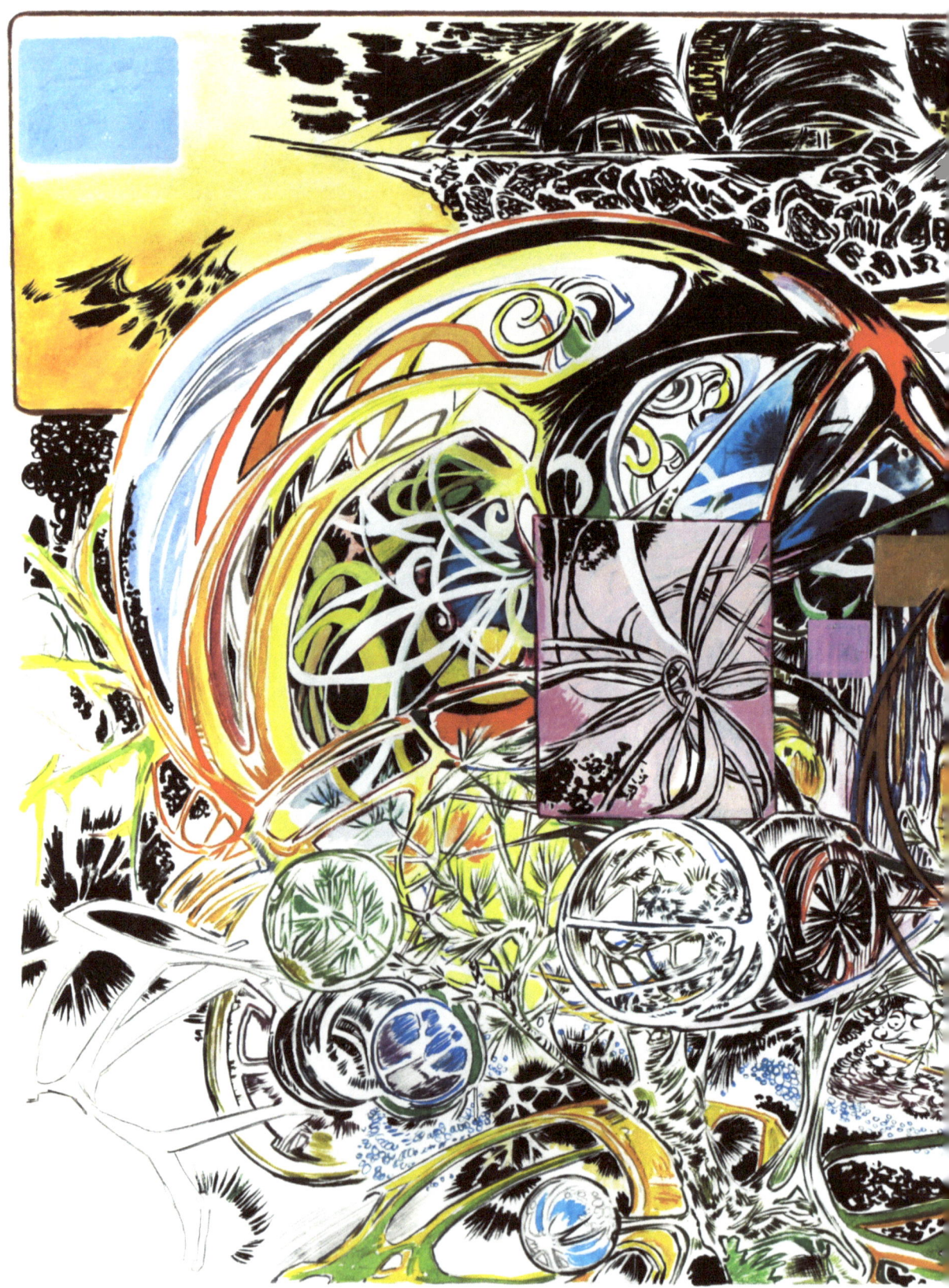

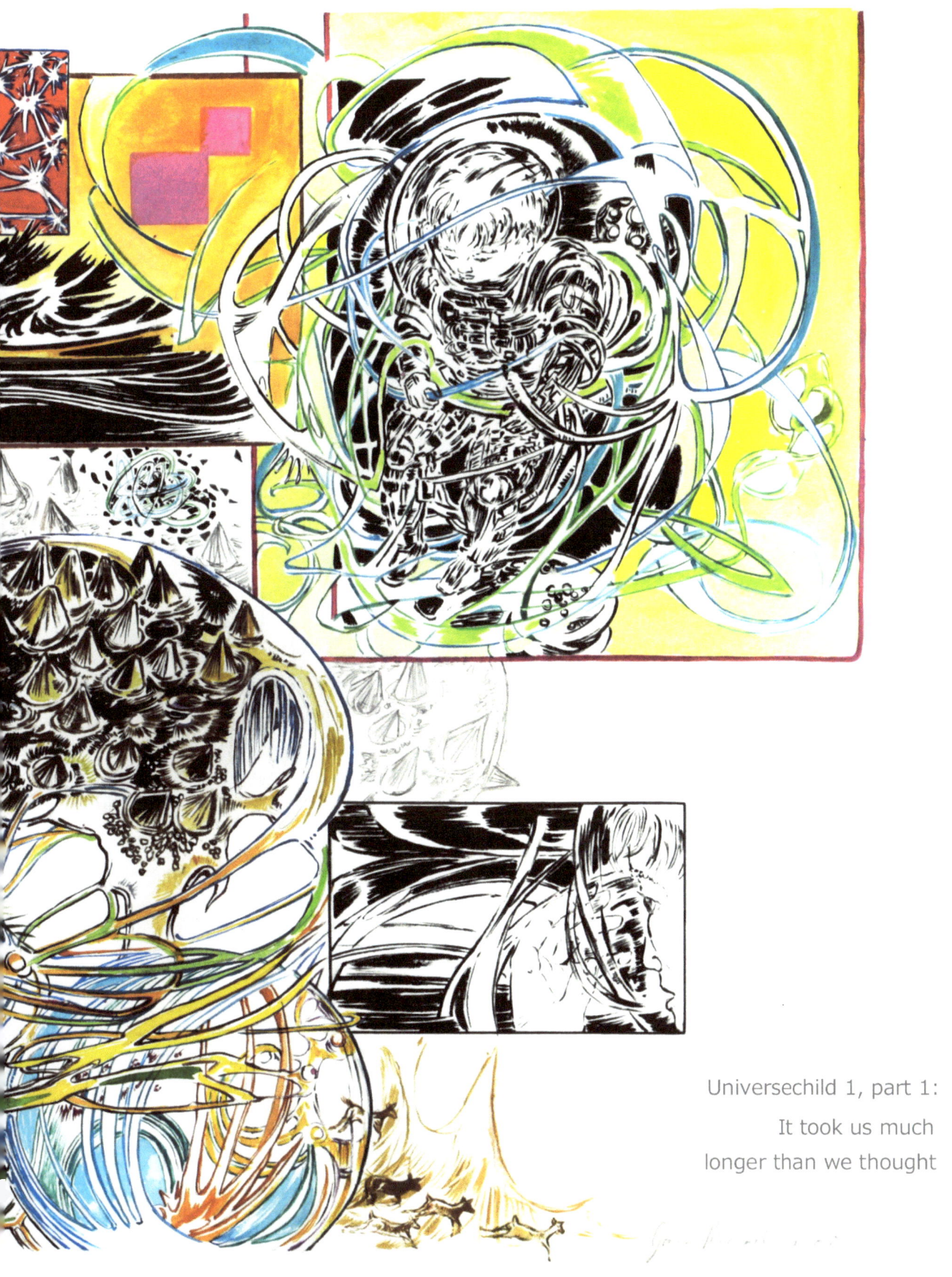

Universechild 1, part 1:
It took us much
longer than we thought

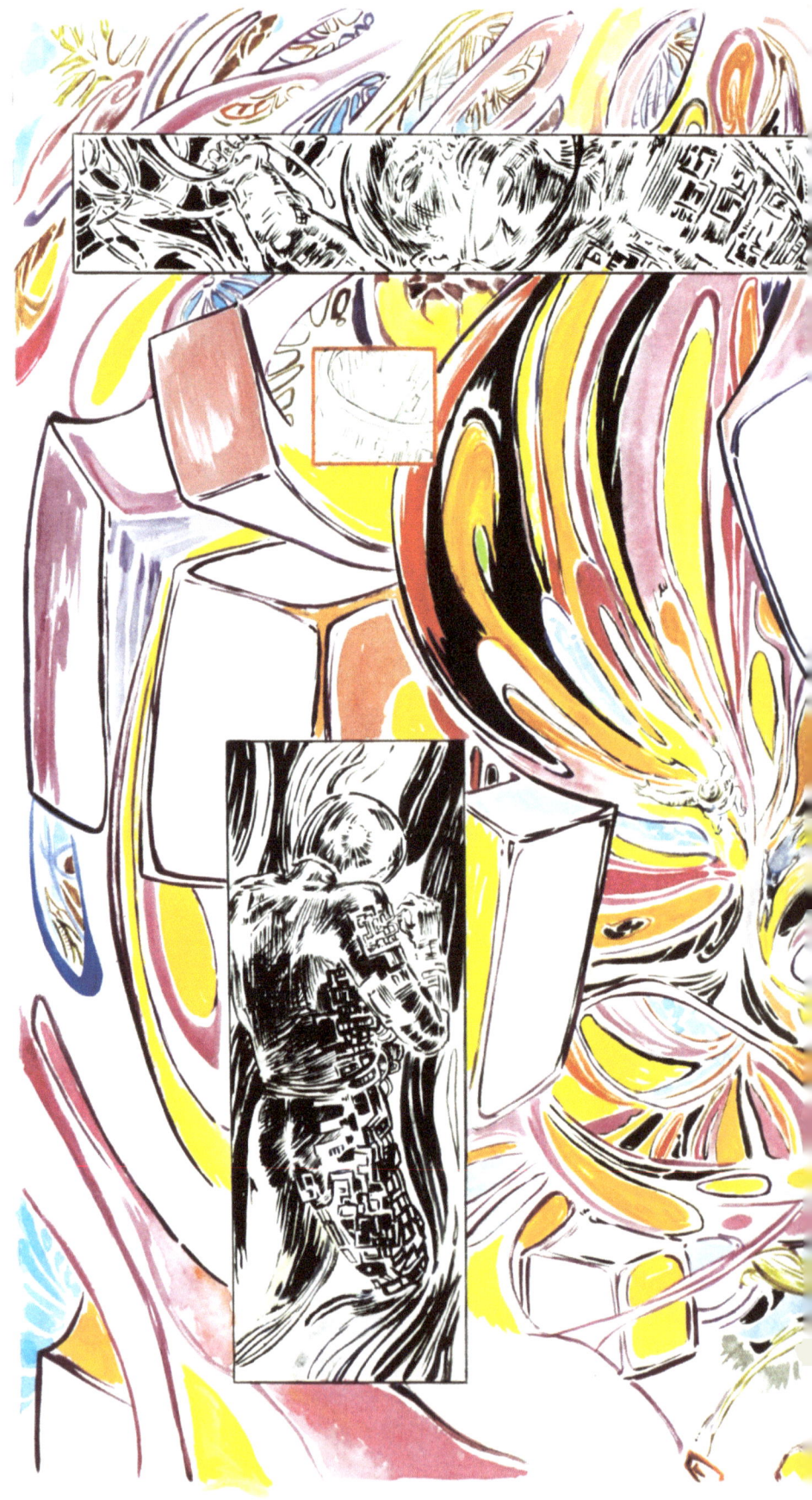

Universechild 1, part 2:

into the Universechild

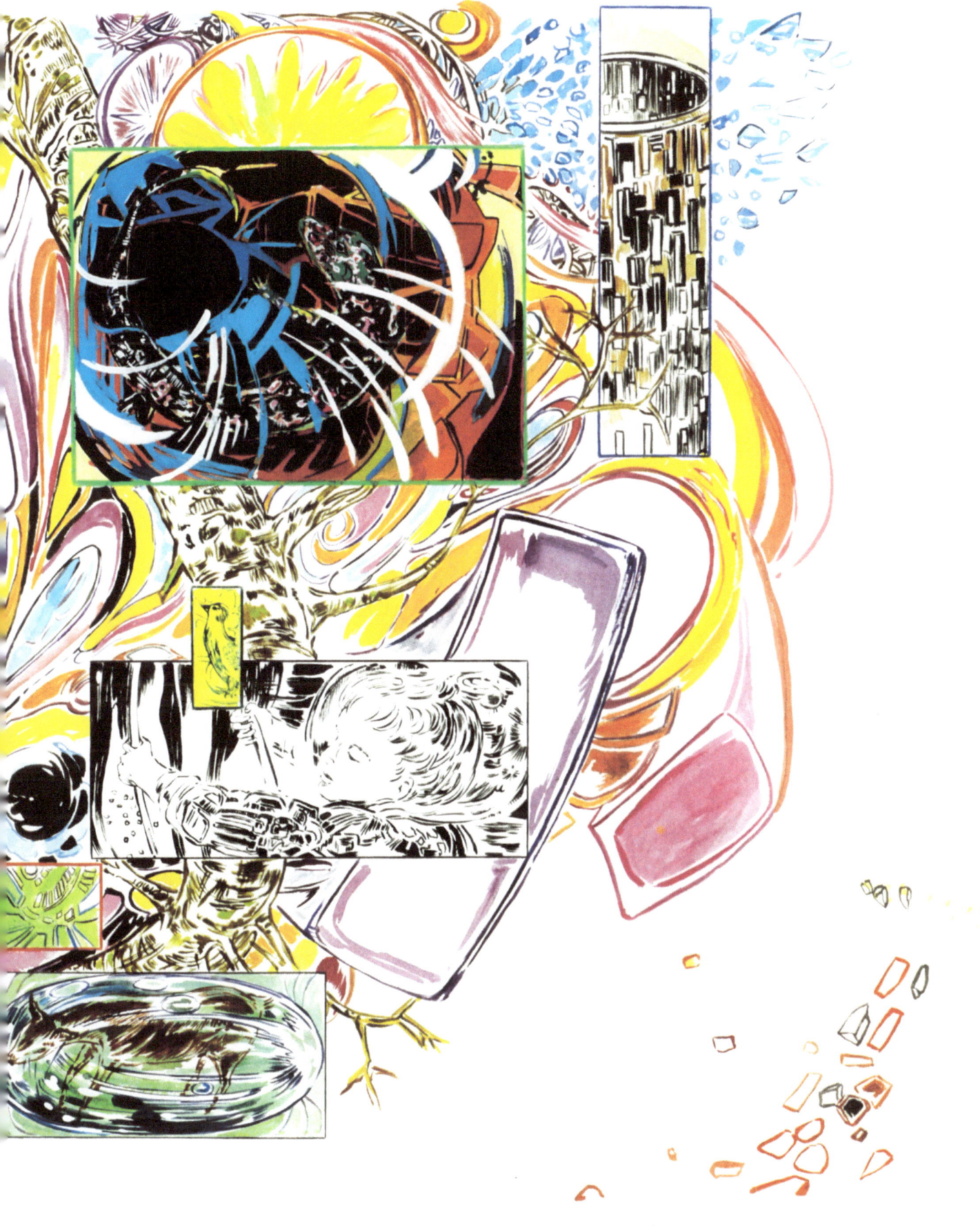

Universechild 2:

we could have anything we wanted and everything
become real so we no longer wanted anything

(detail)

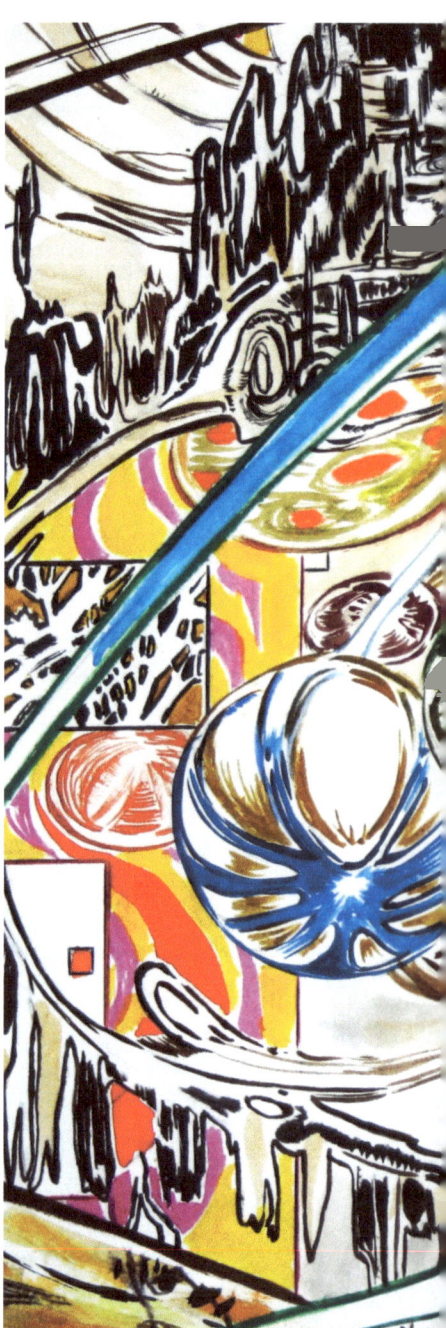

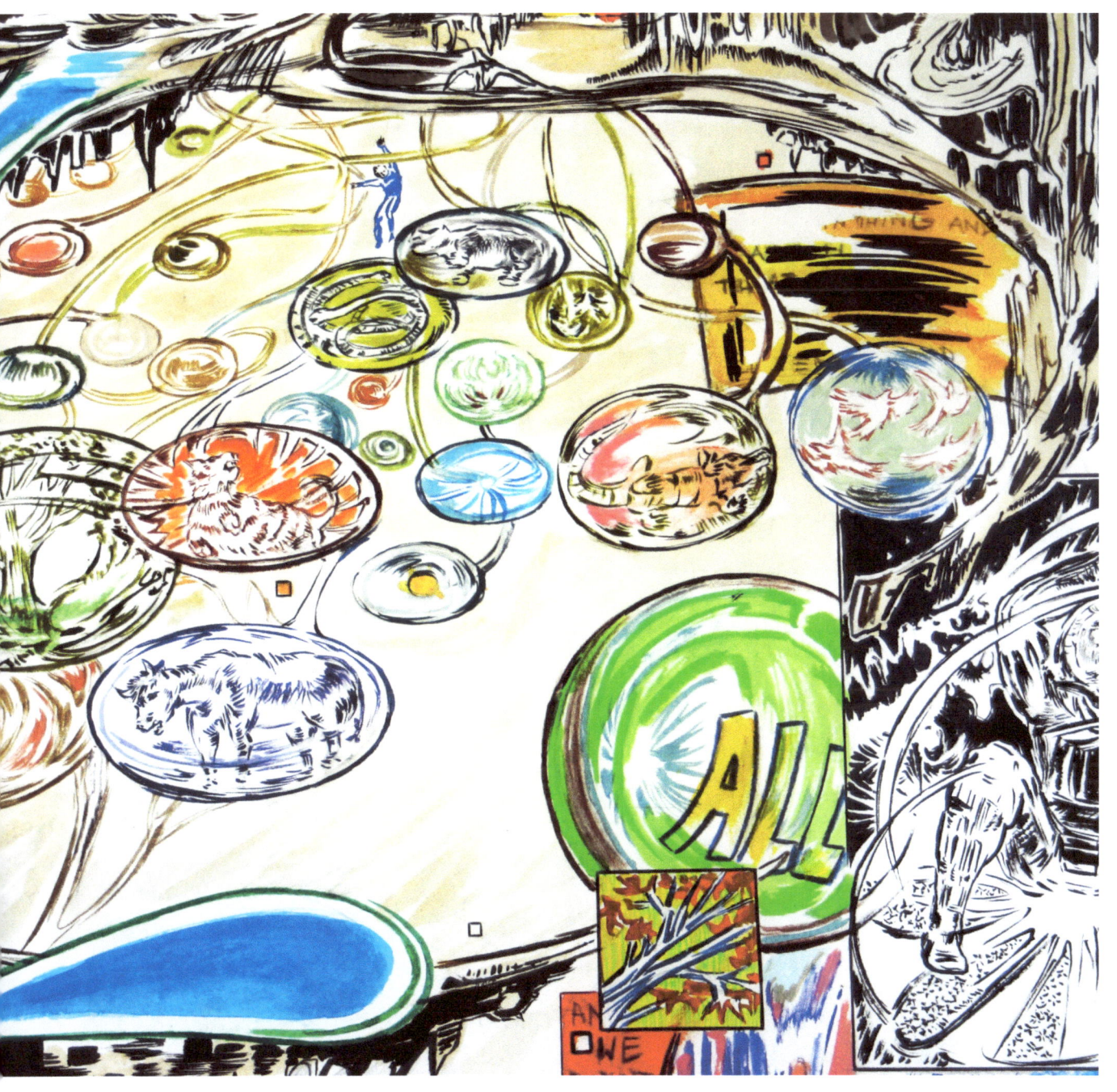

overleaf: Universechild 2 >

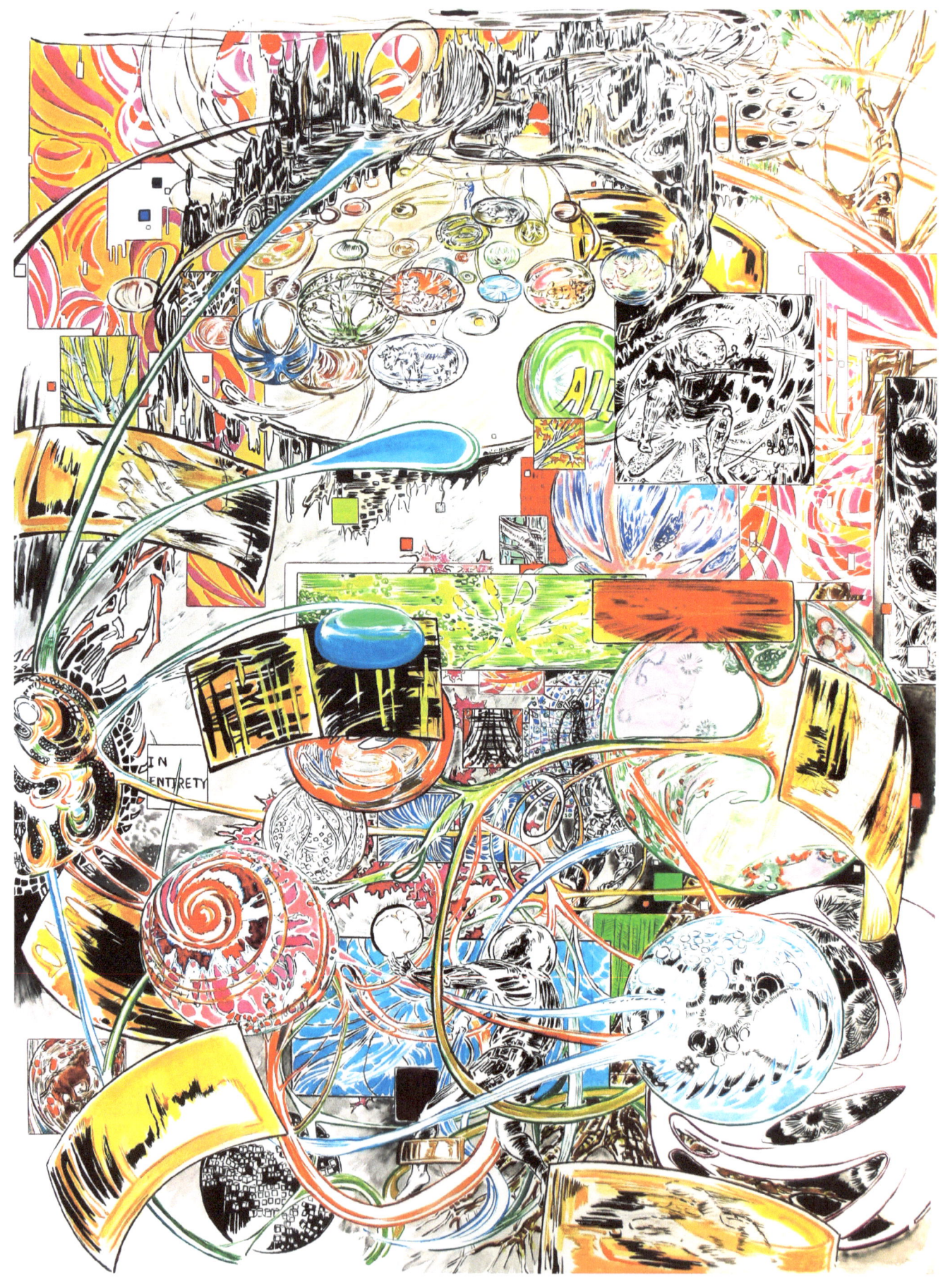

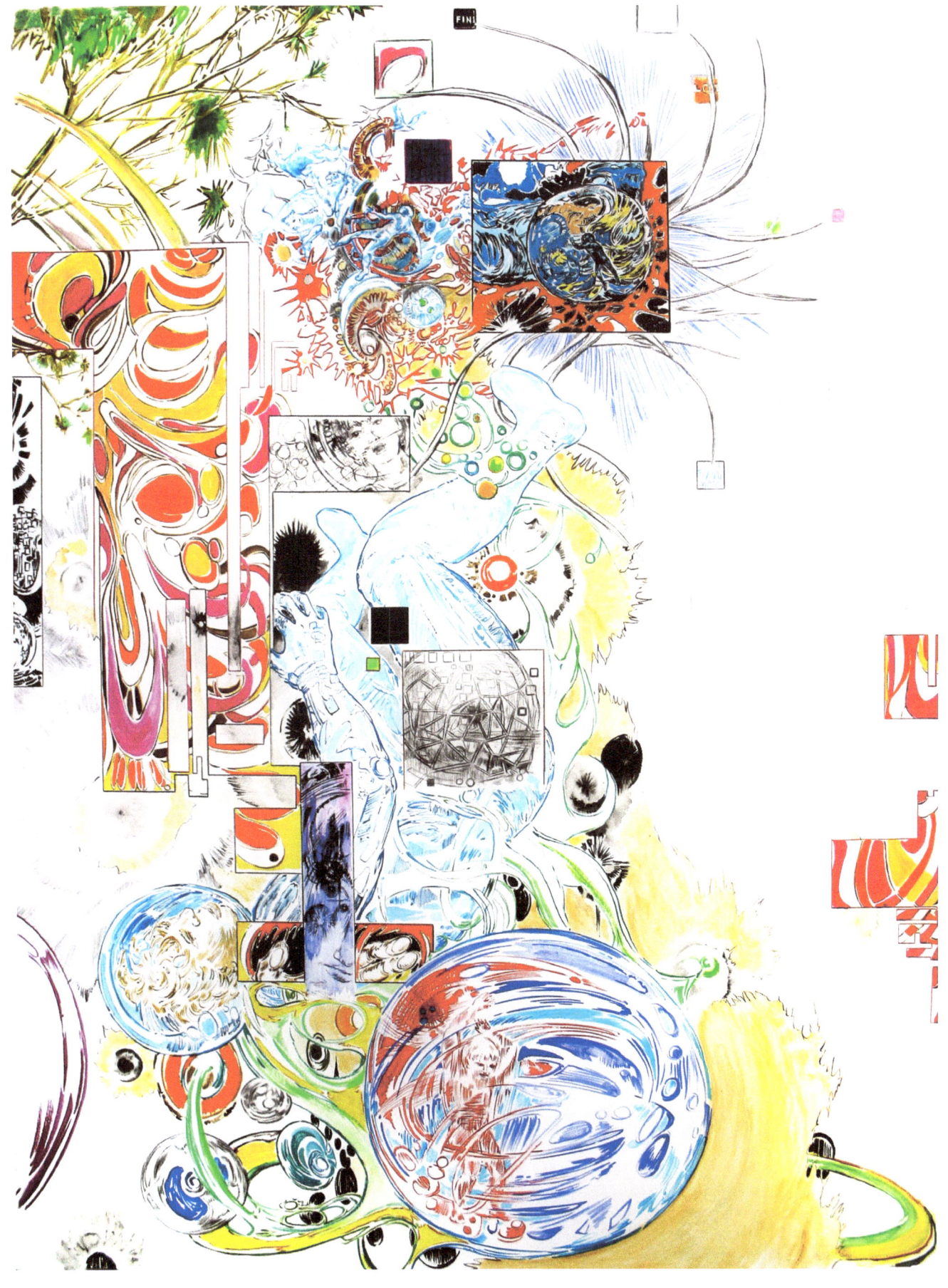

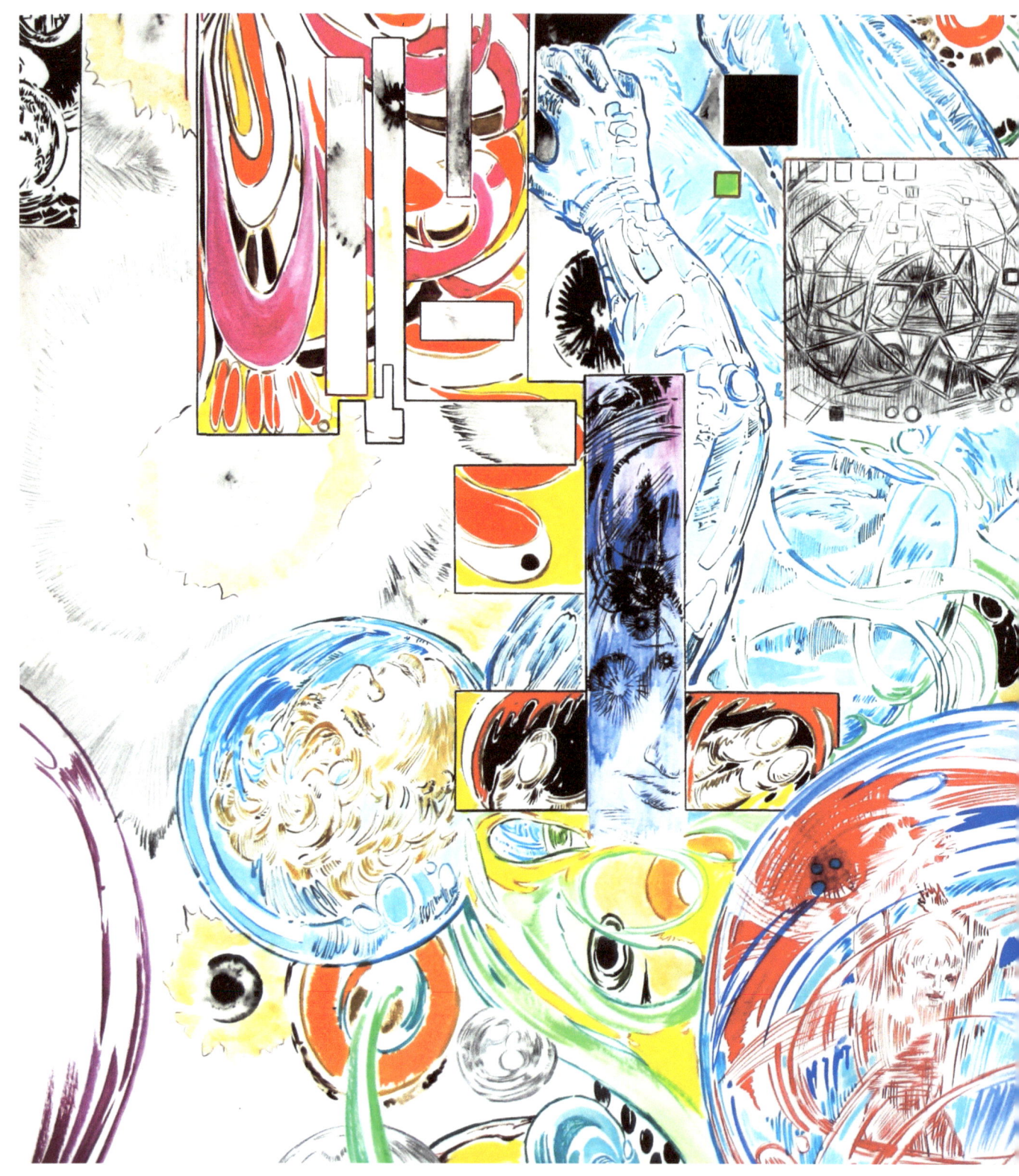

< overleaf: Universechild 3:
everything here is alive and everything is here

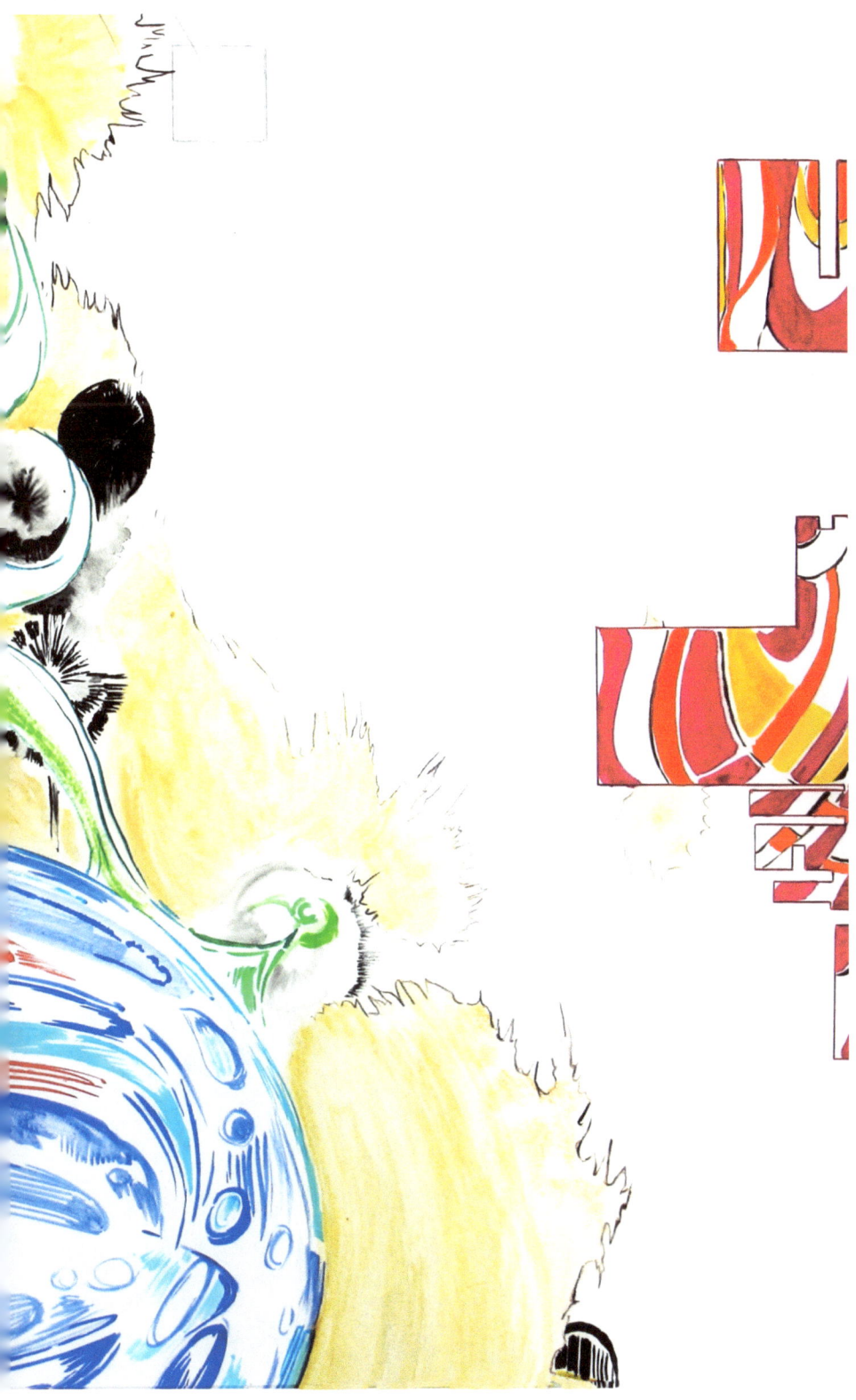

Universechild 3
(detail)

Universechild 4:
we thought
it would
be wonderful

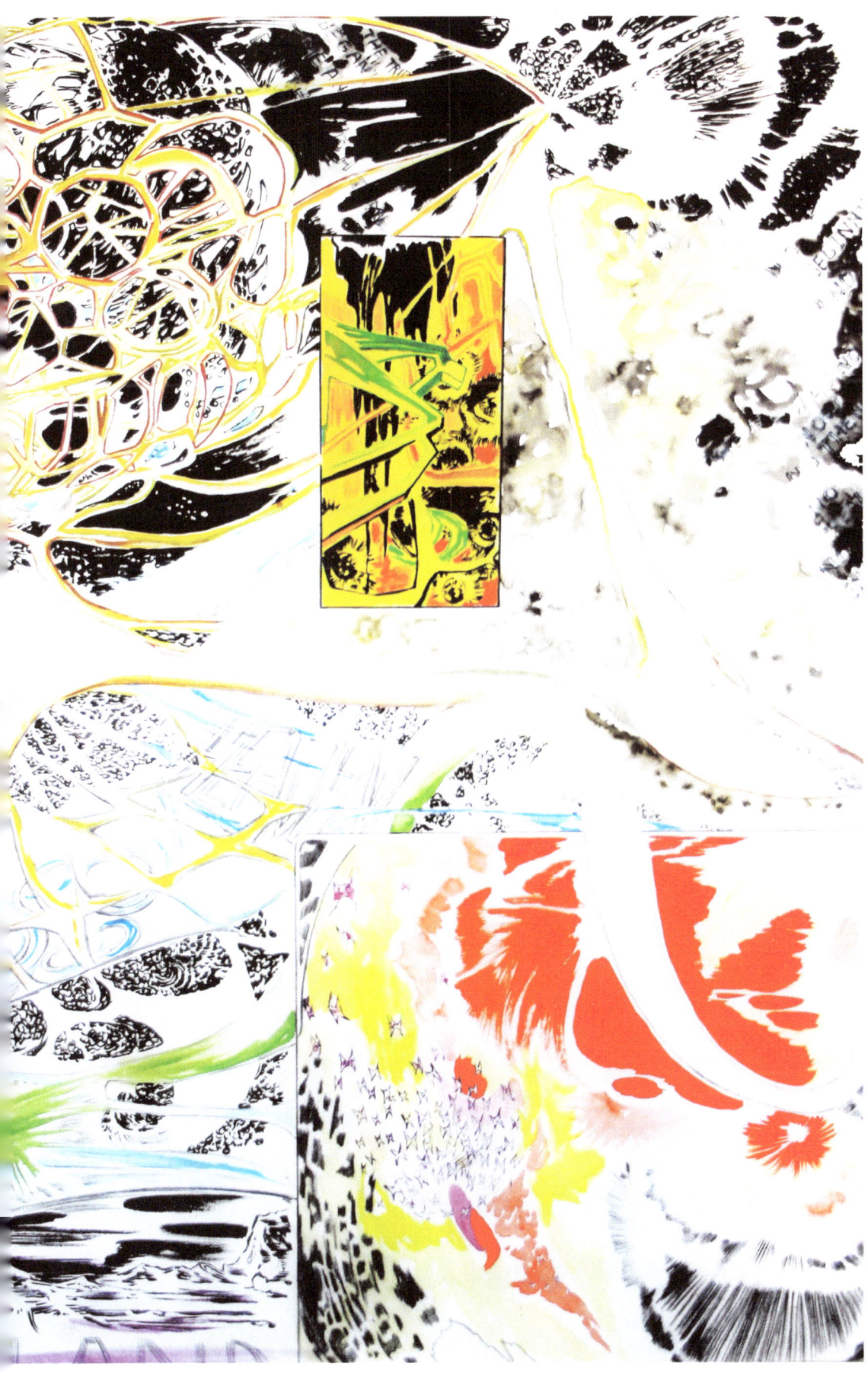

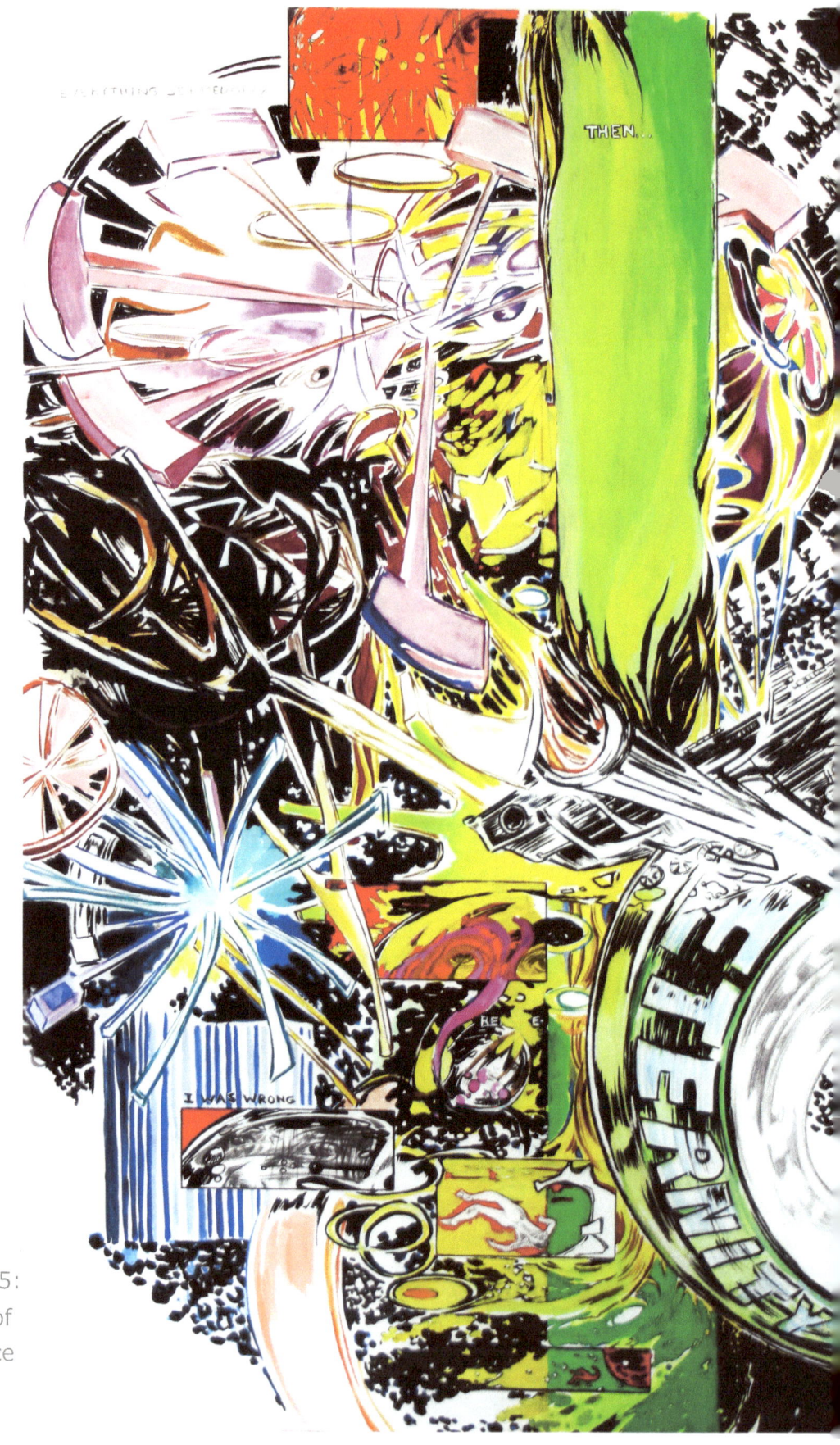

Universechild 5:
eternity of
empty space

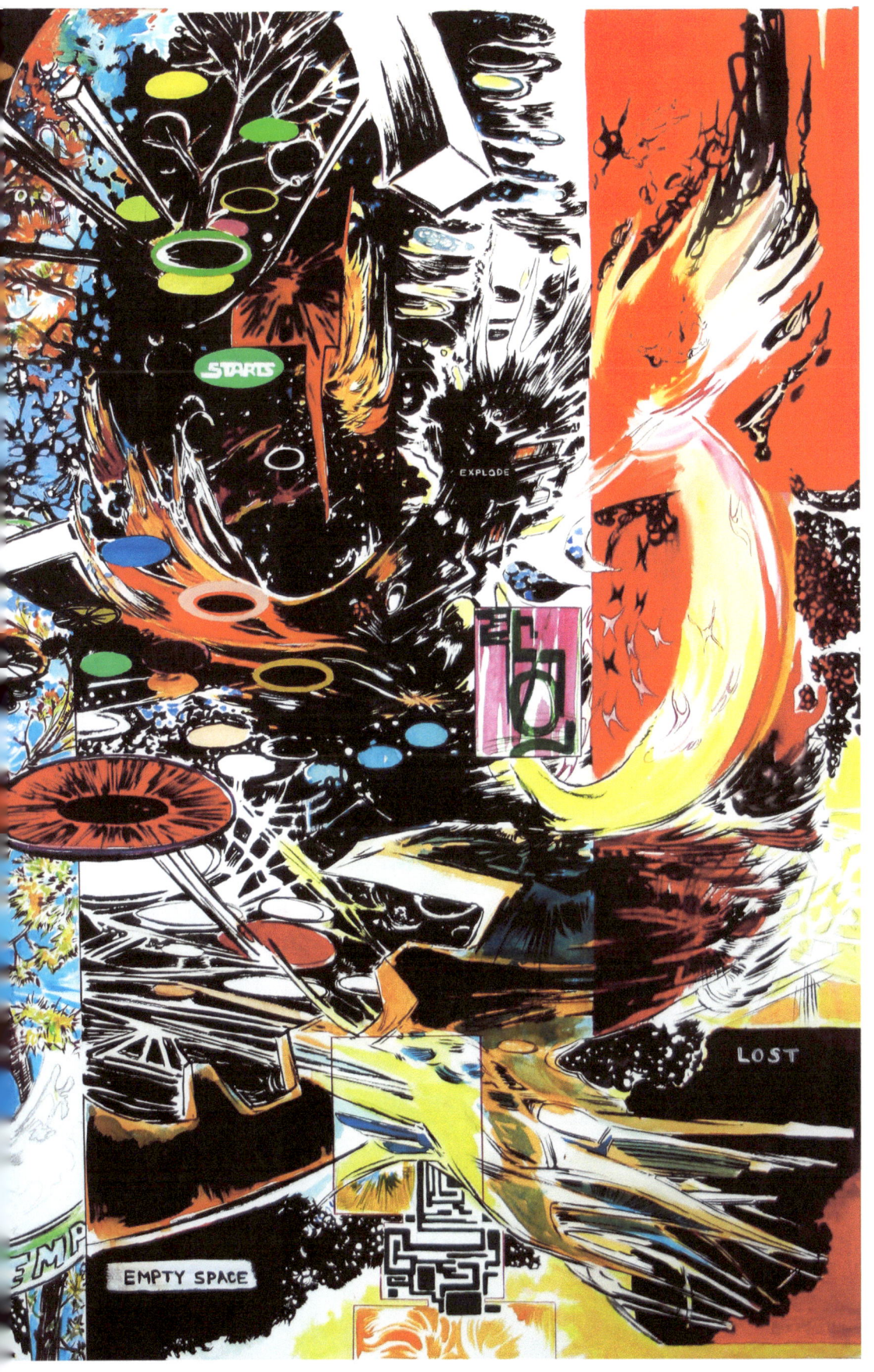

Universechild 6:
never shoot a gun
in outer space

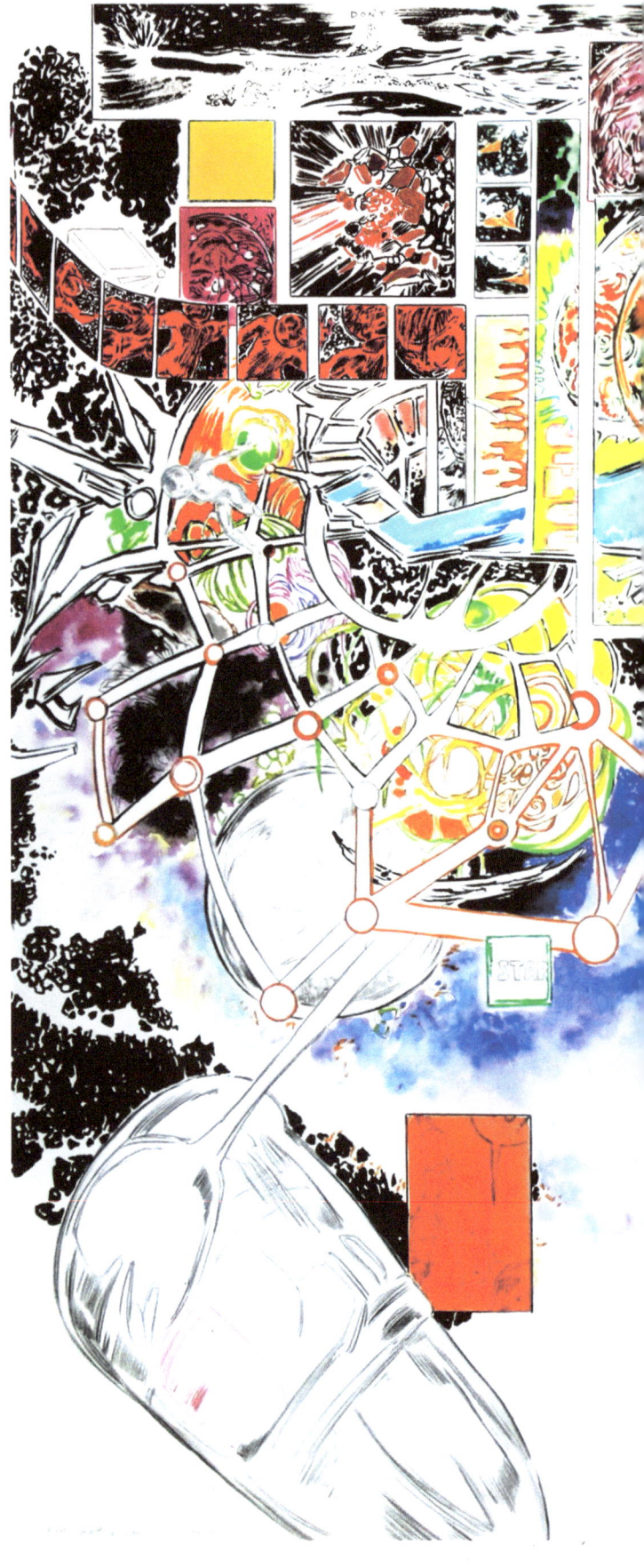

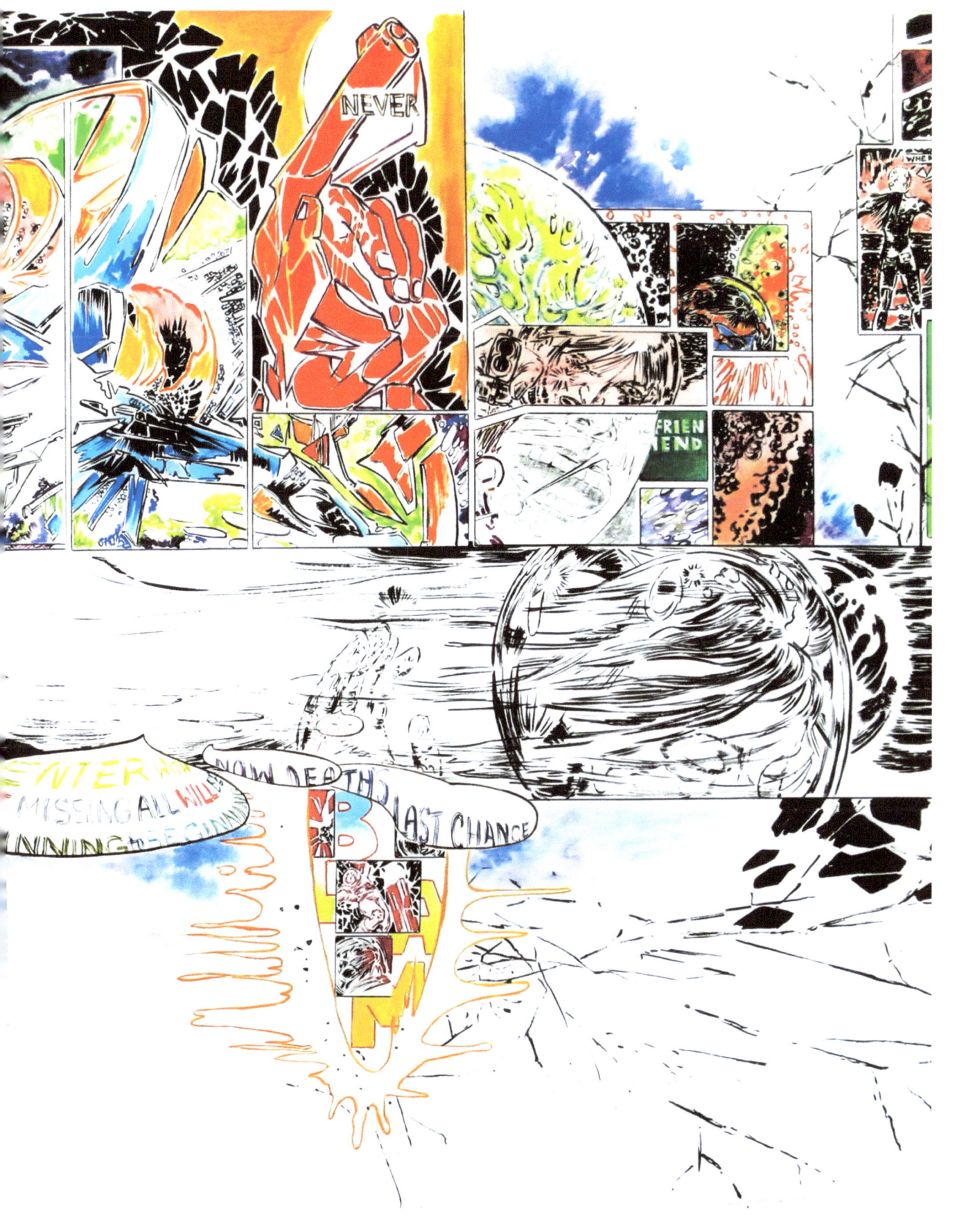

Universechild 6
(detail)

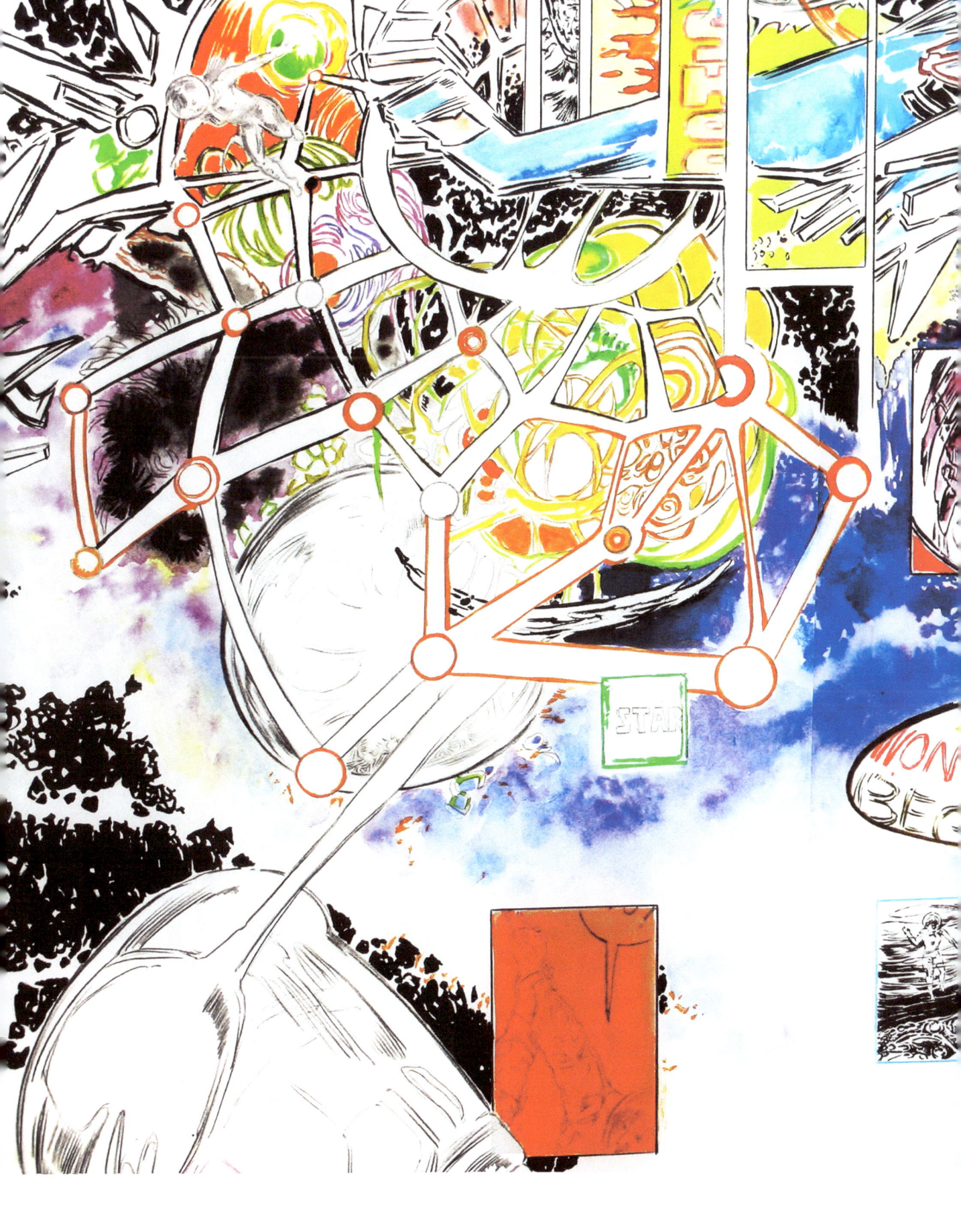

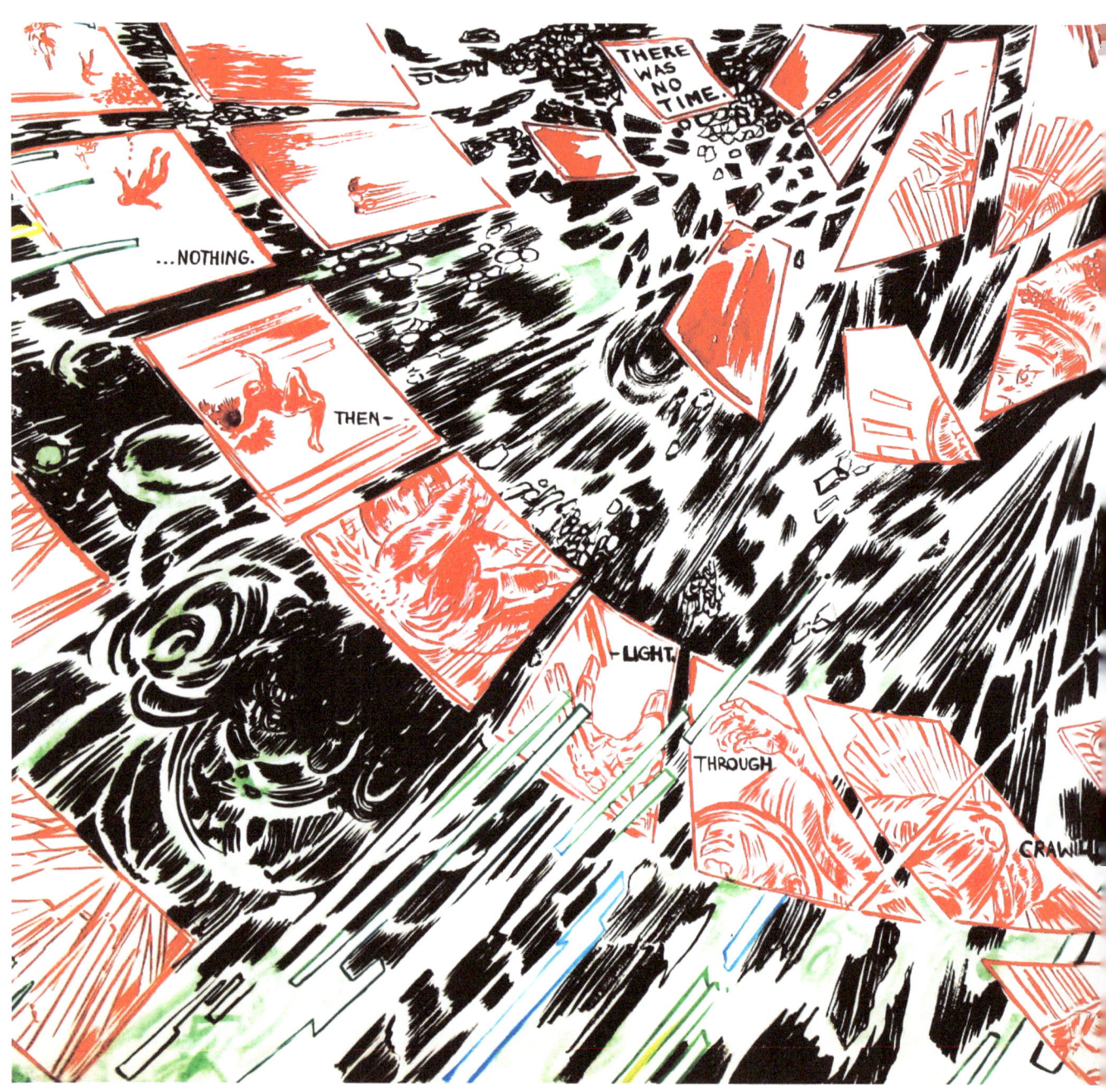

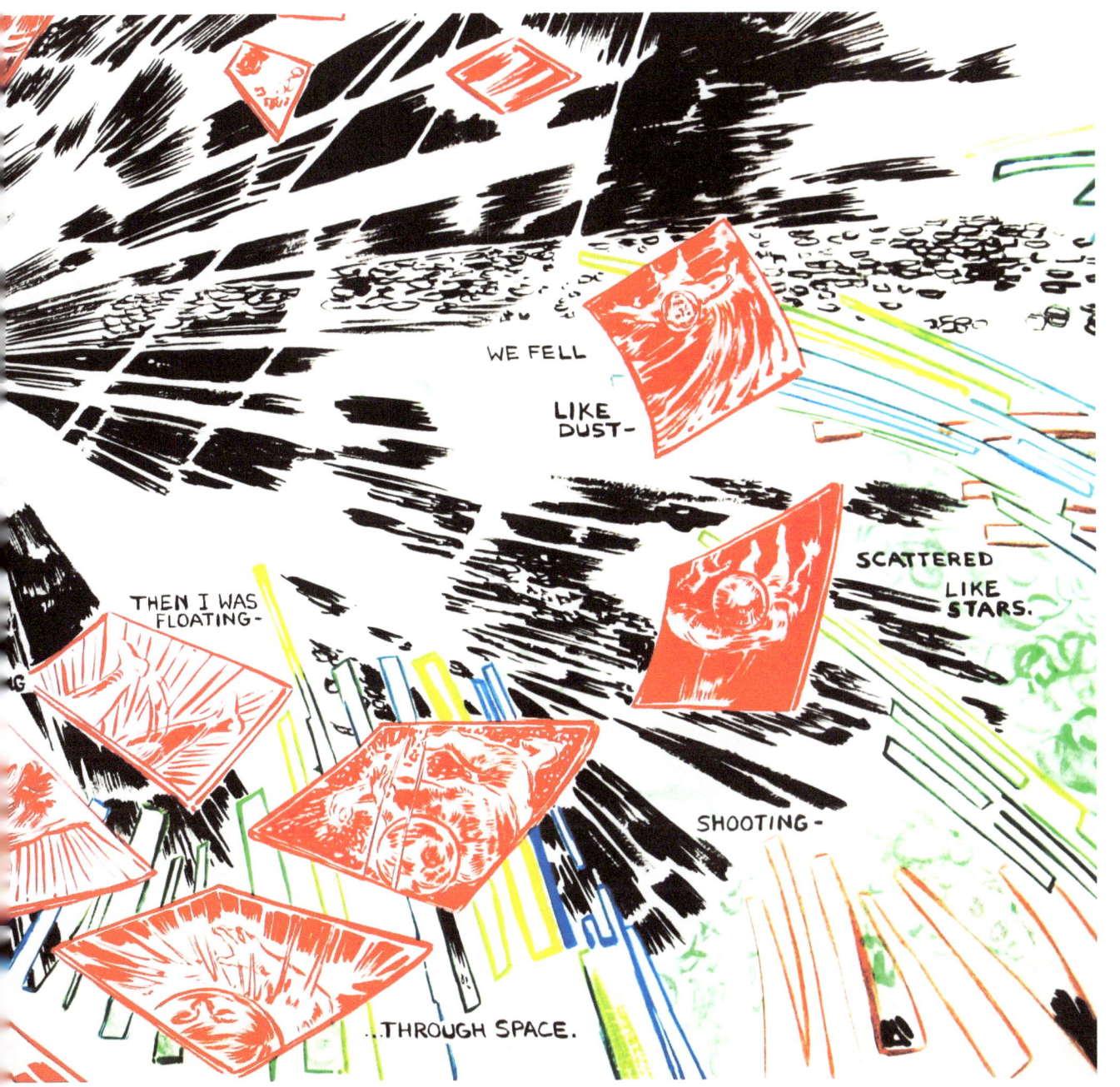

Universechild 7:
no time

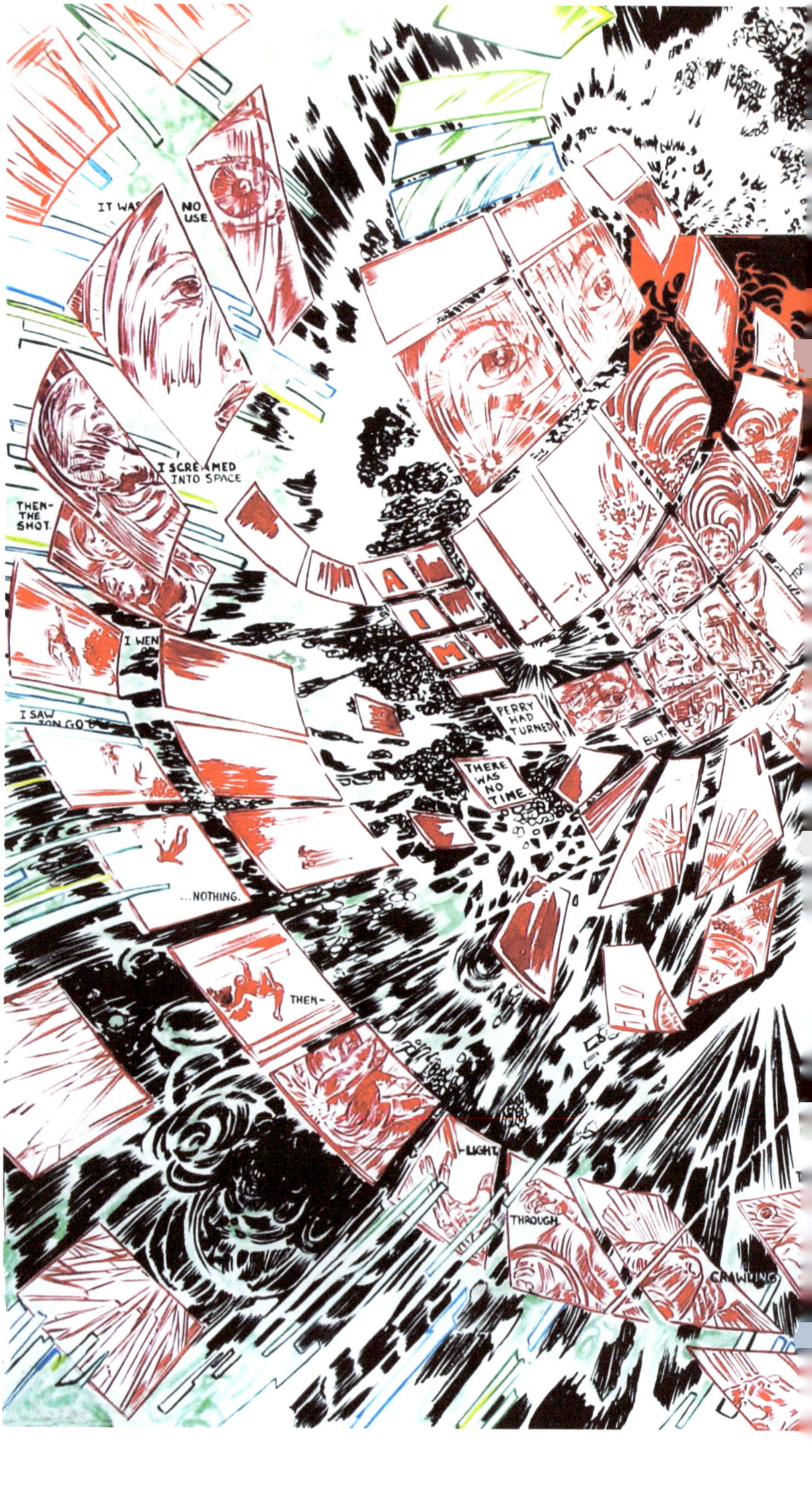

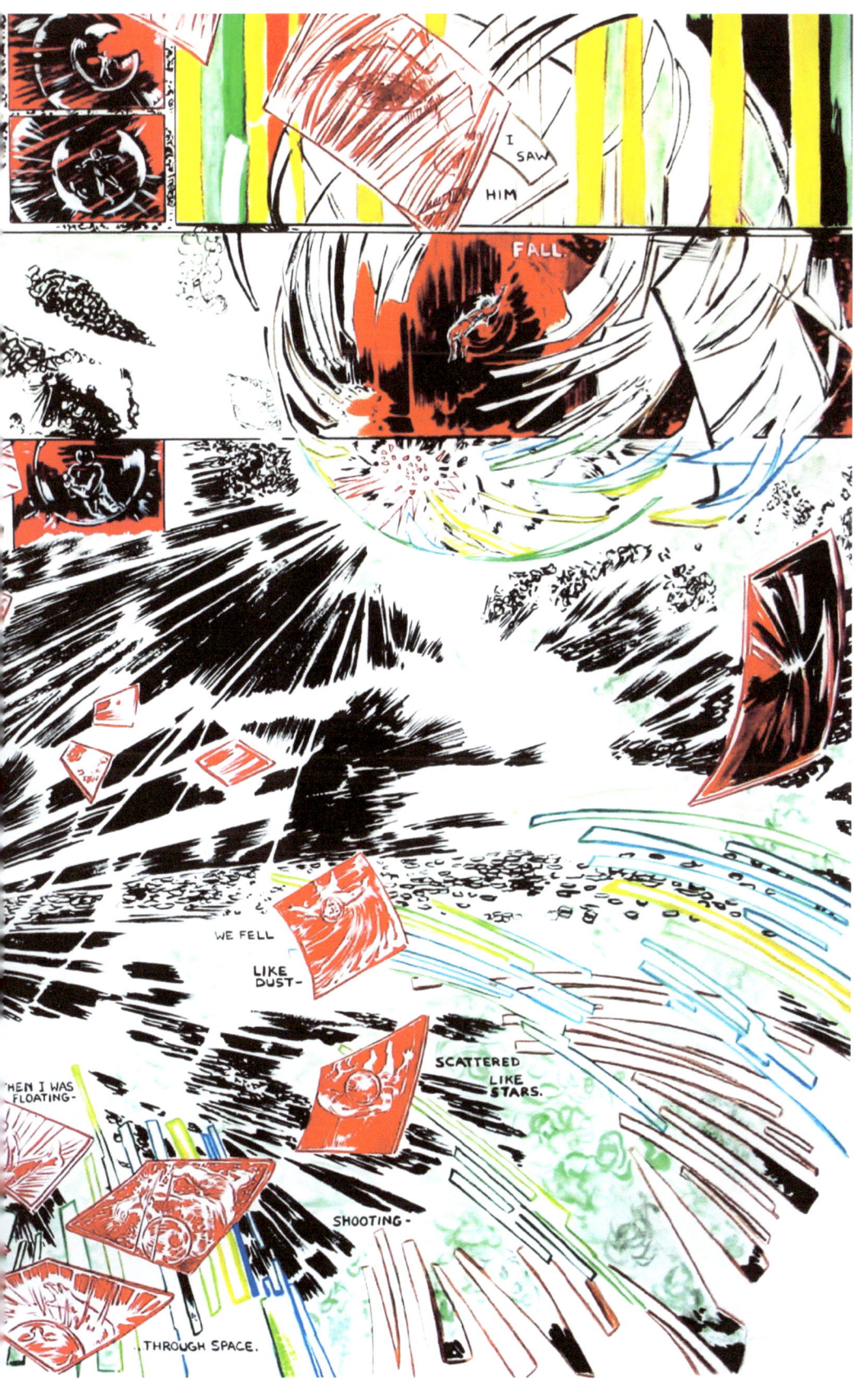

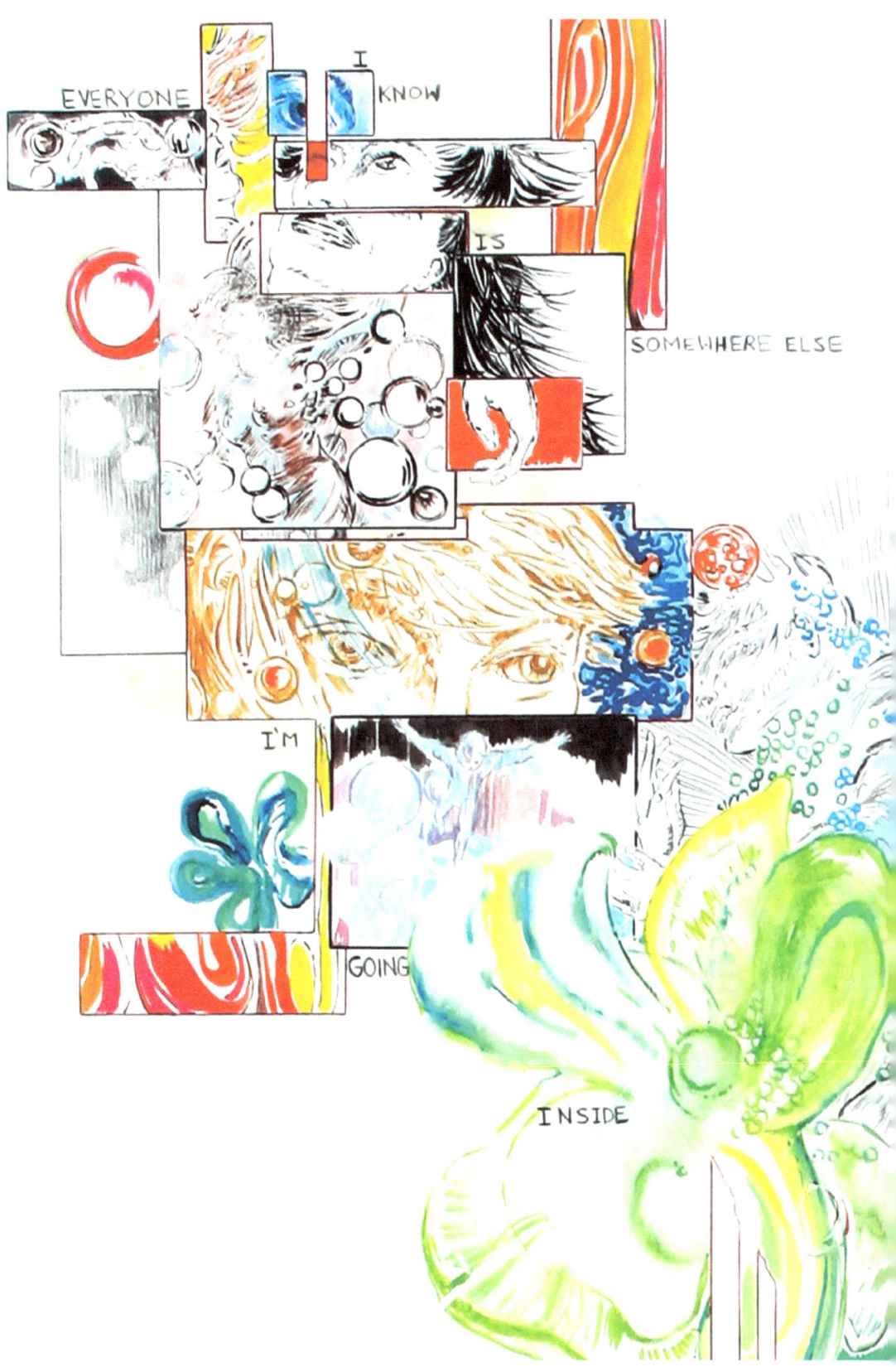

Universechild 8:
everyone I know is somewhere else
(detail)

overleaf > Universechild 8

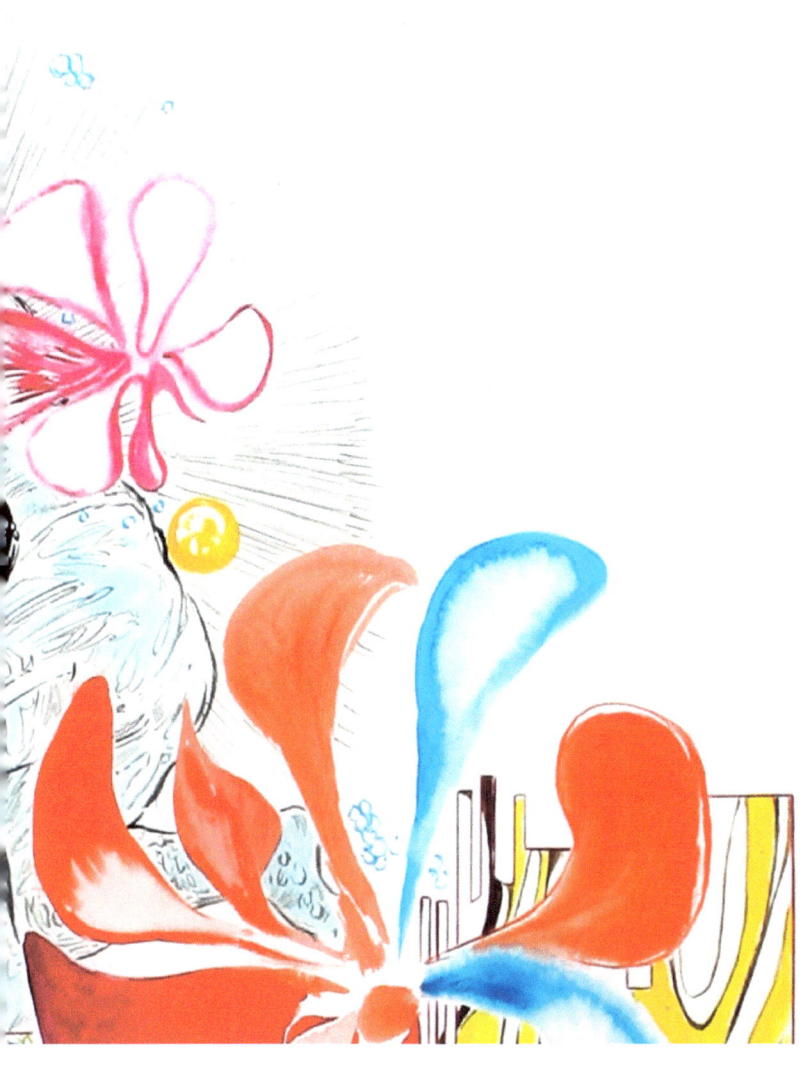

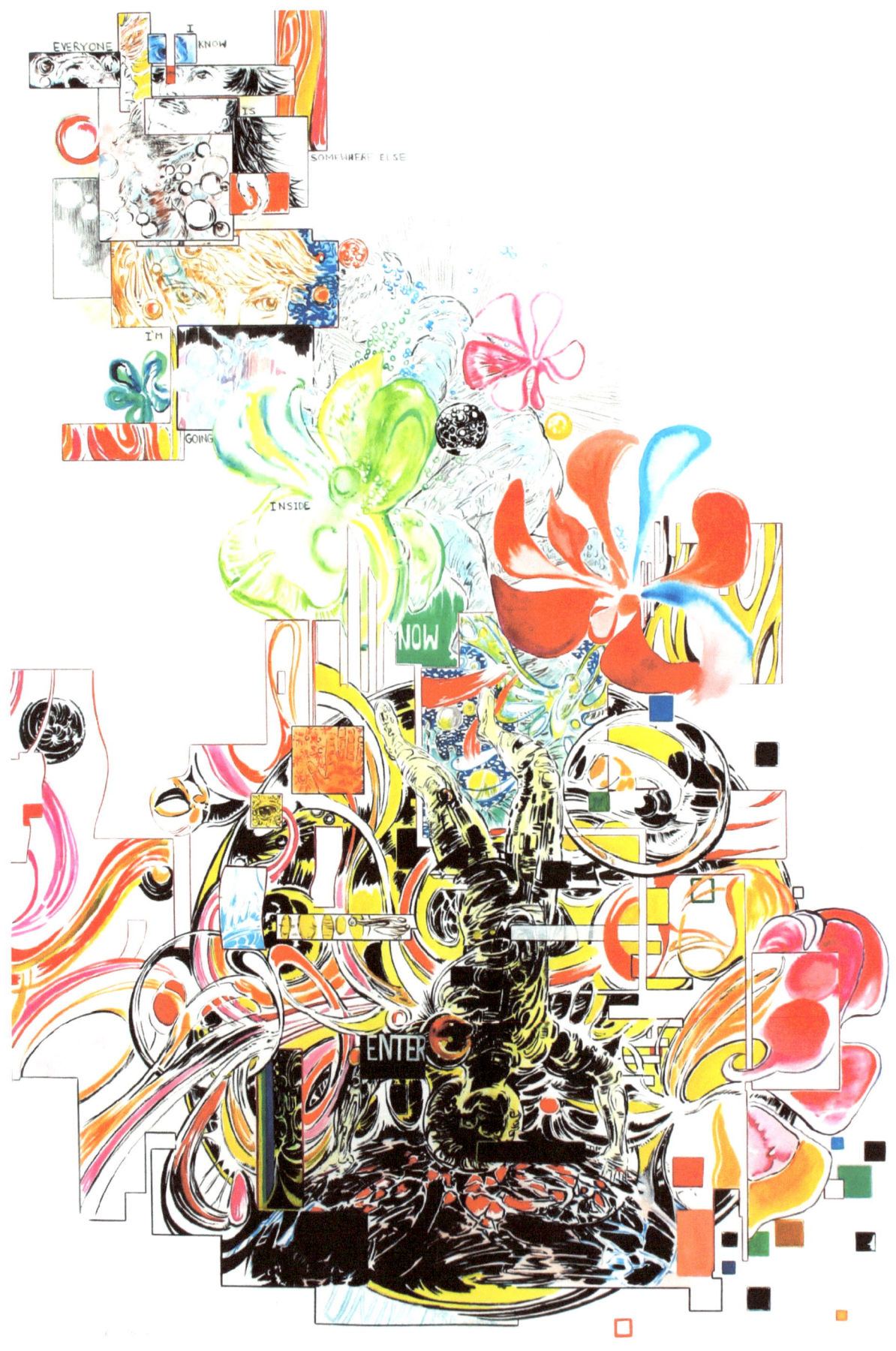

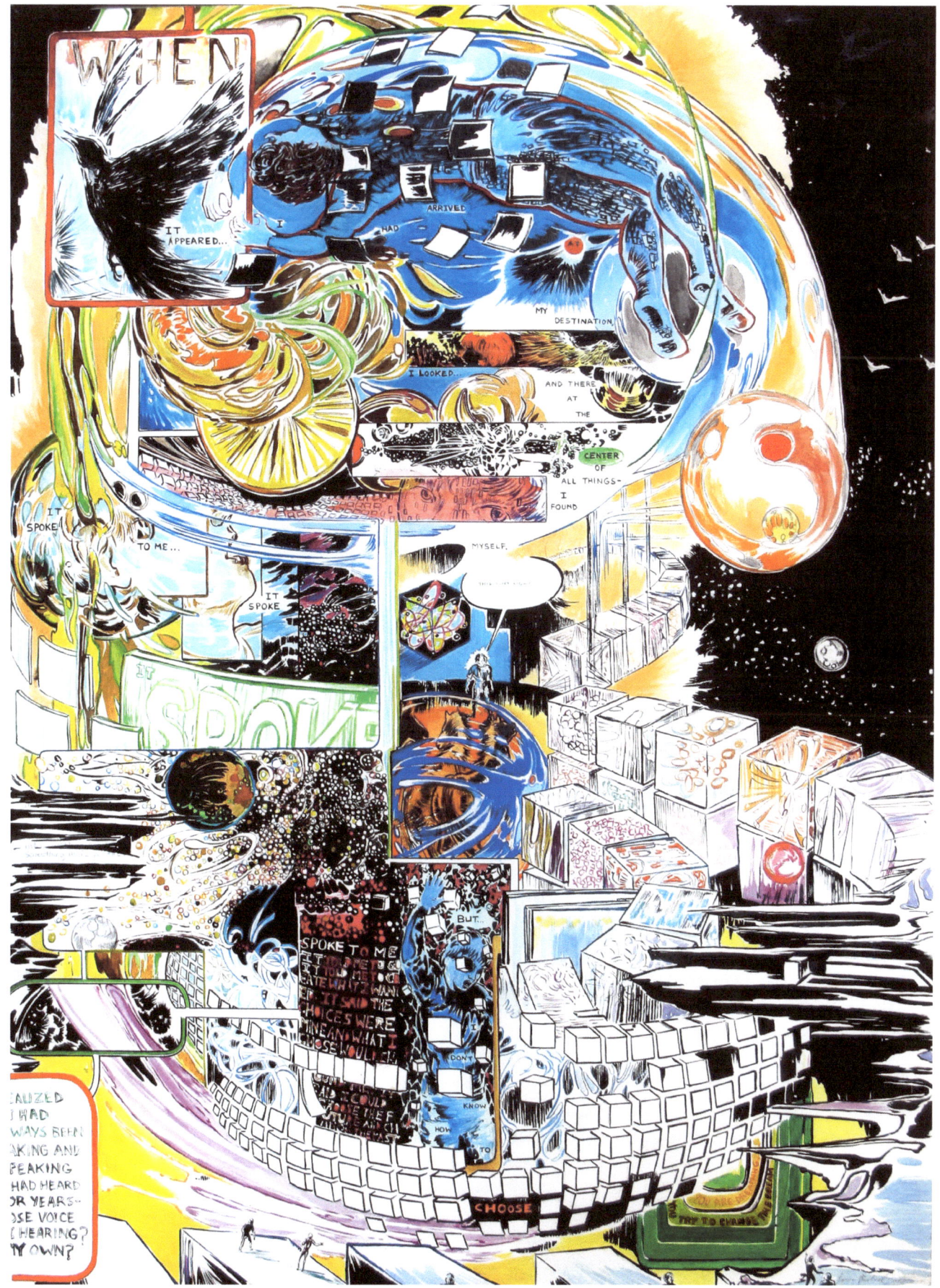

Universechild 9: sometimes you know you are dreaming and you try to change the dream into something better, something more perfect

(detail)

< overleaf: Universechild 9

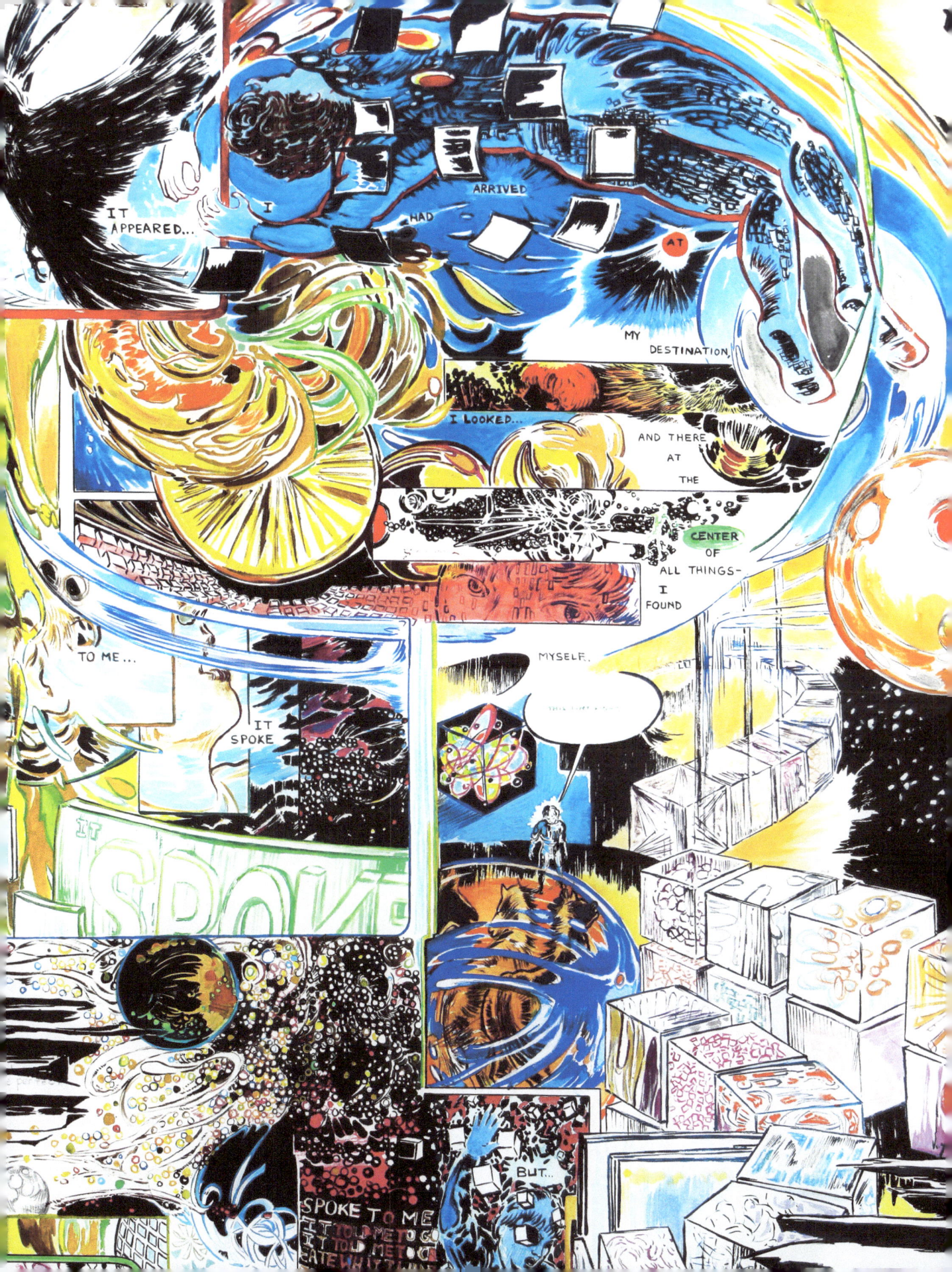

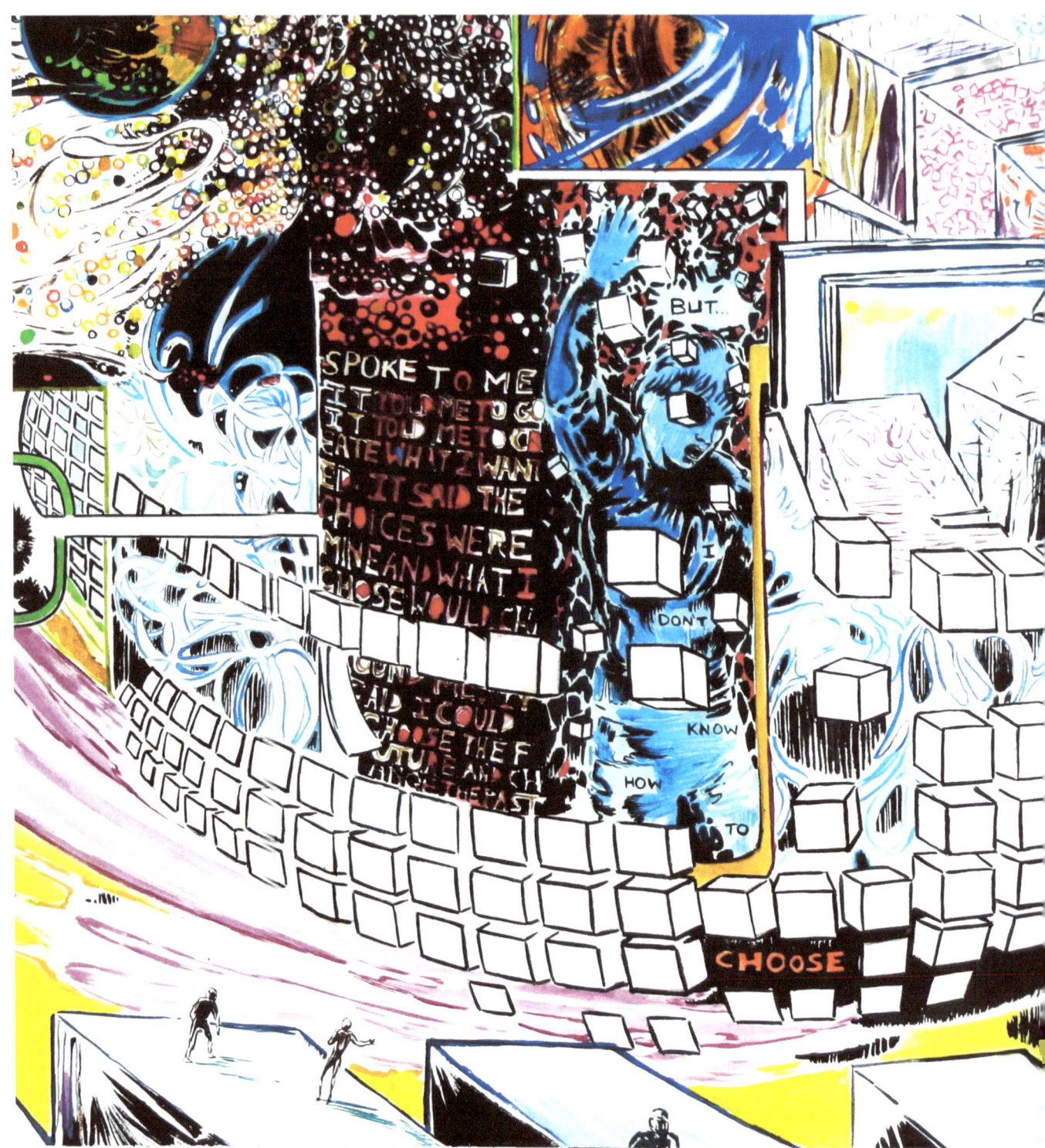

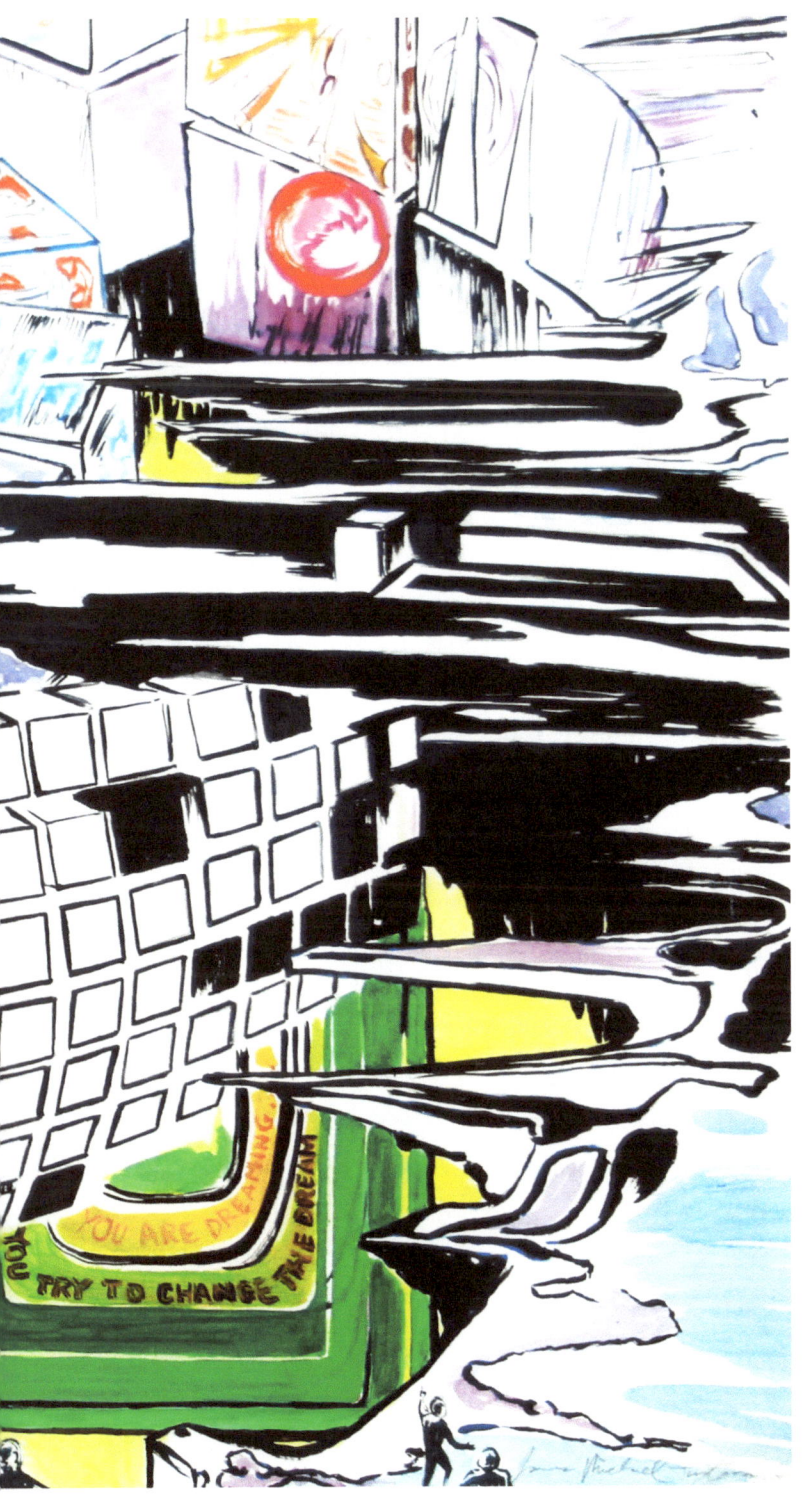

Universechild 9: detail

Universechild 10: open and closed systems (will the city pay for this?)   (detail)

Following pages: Universechild 10

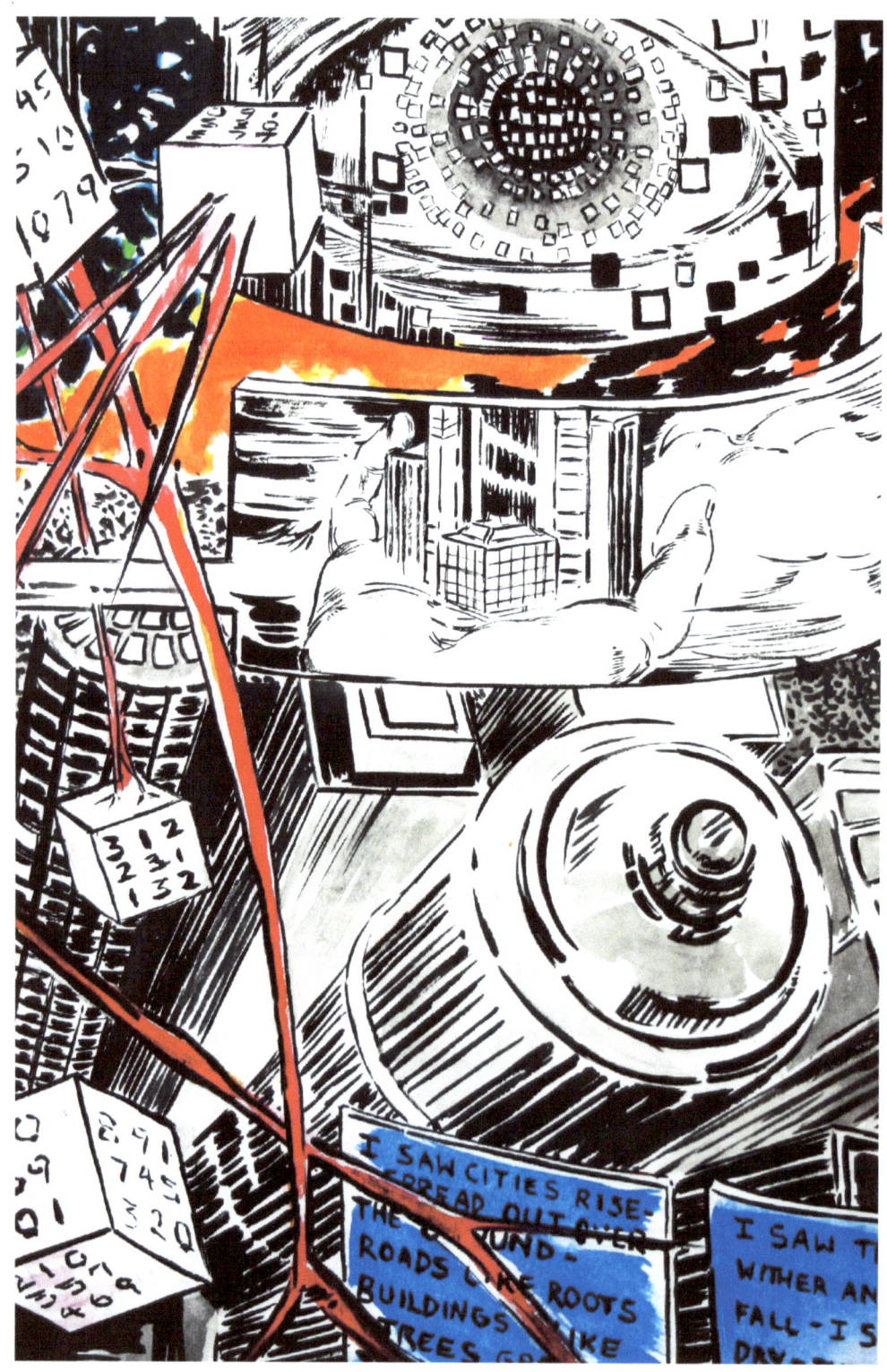

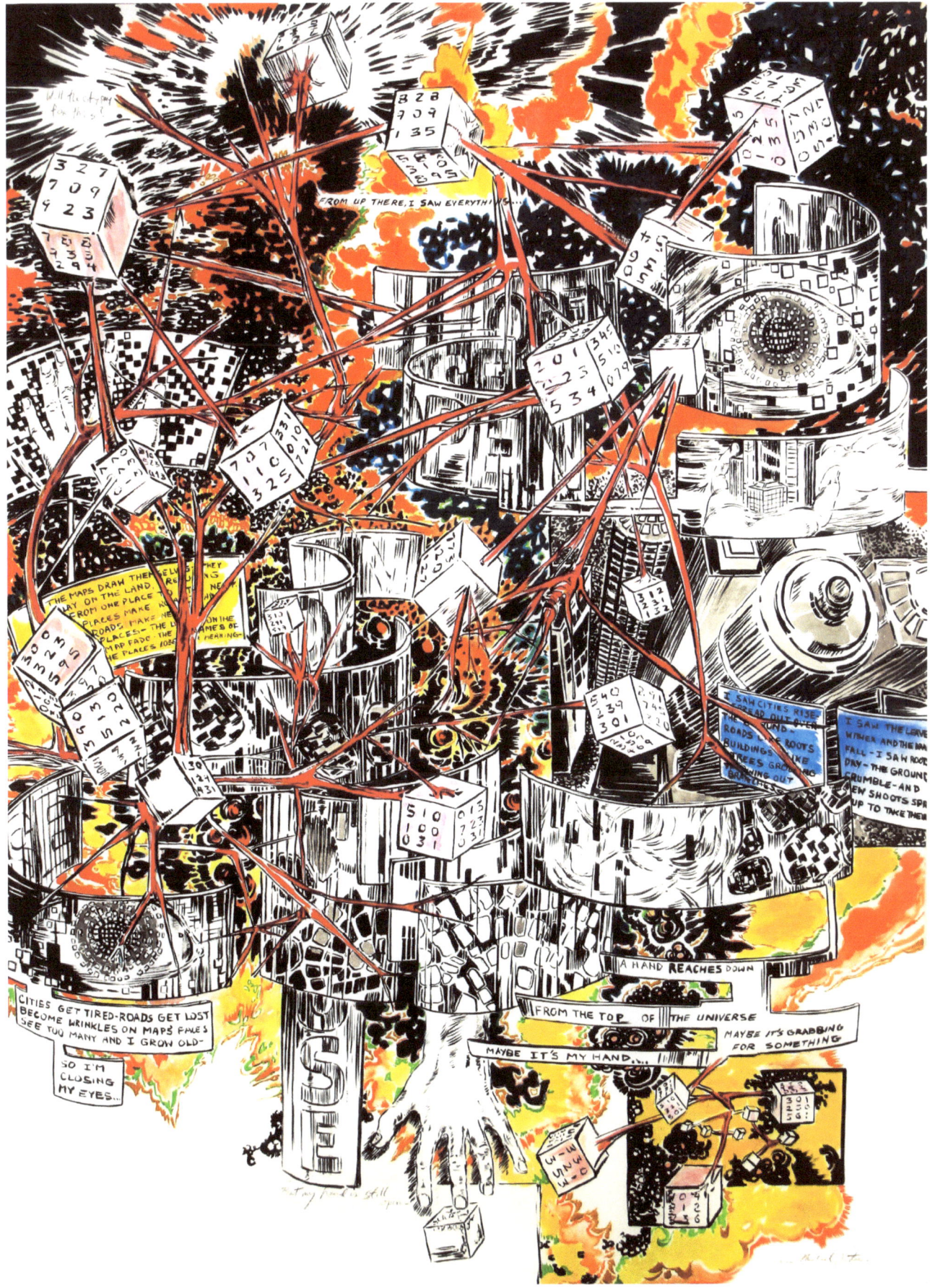

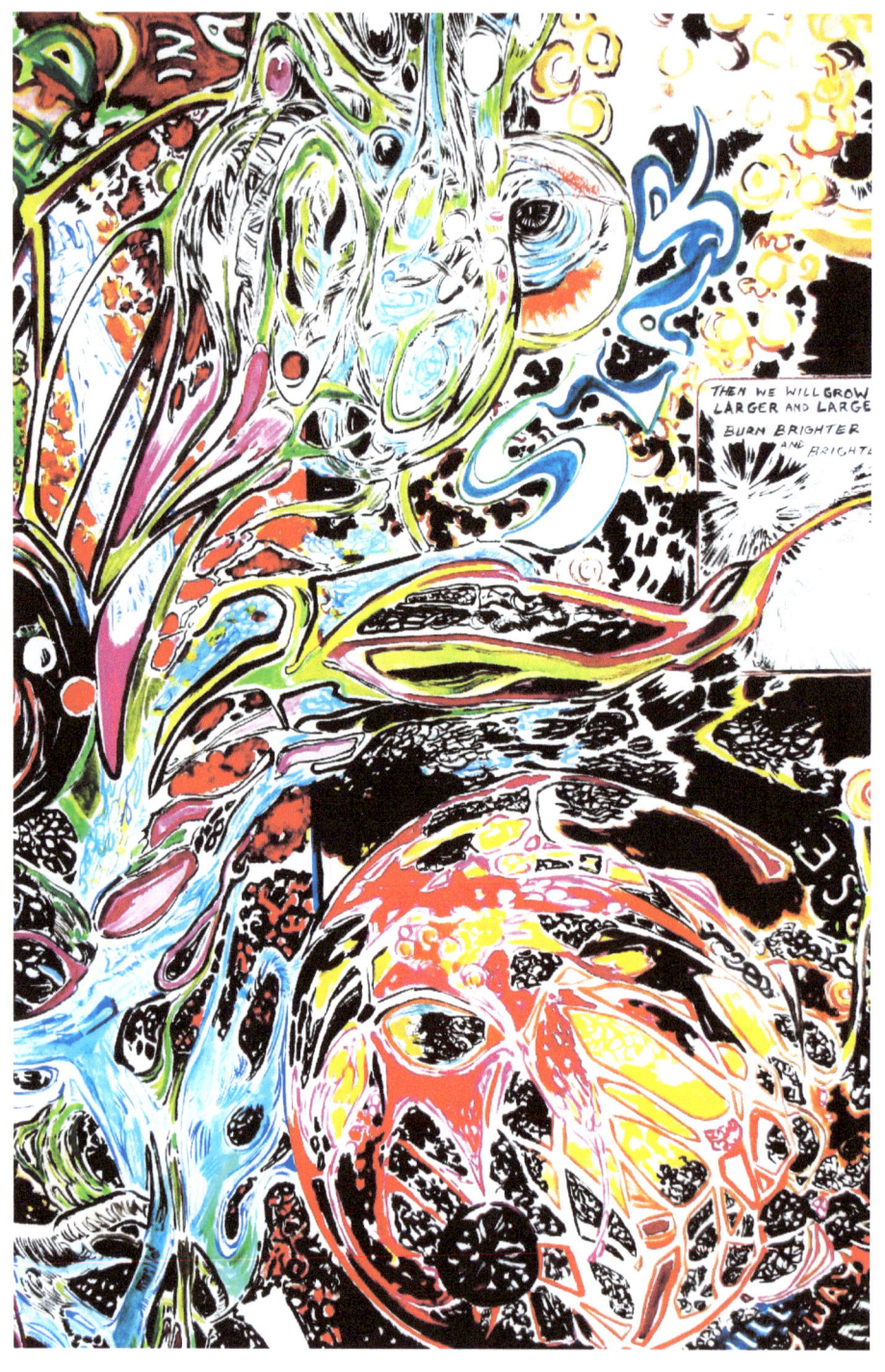

Universechild 11: planted like seeds in a star (details)

overleaf: Universechild 11 >

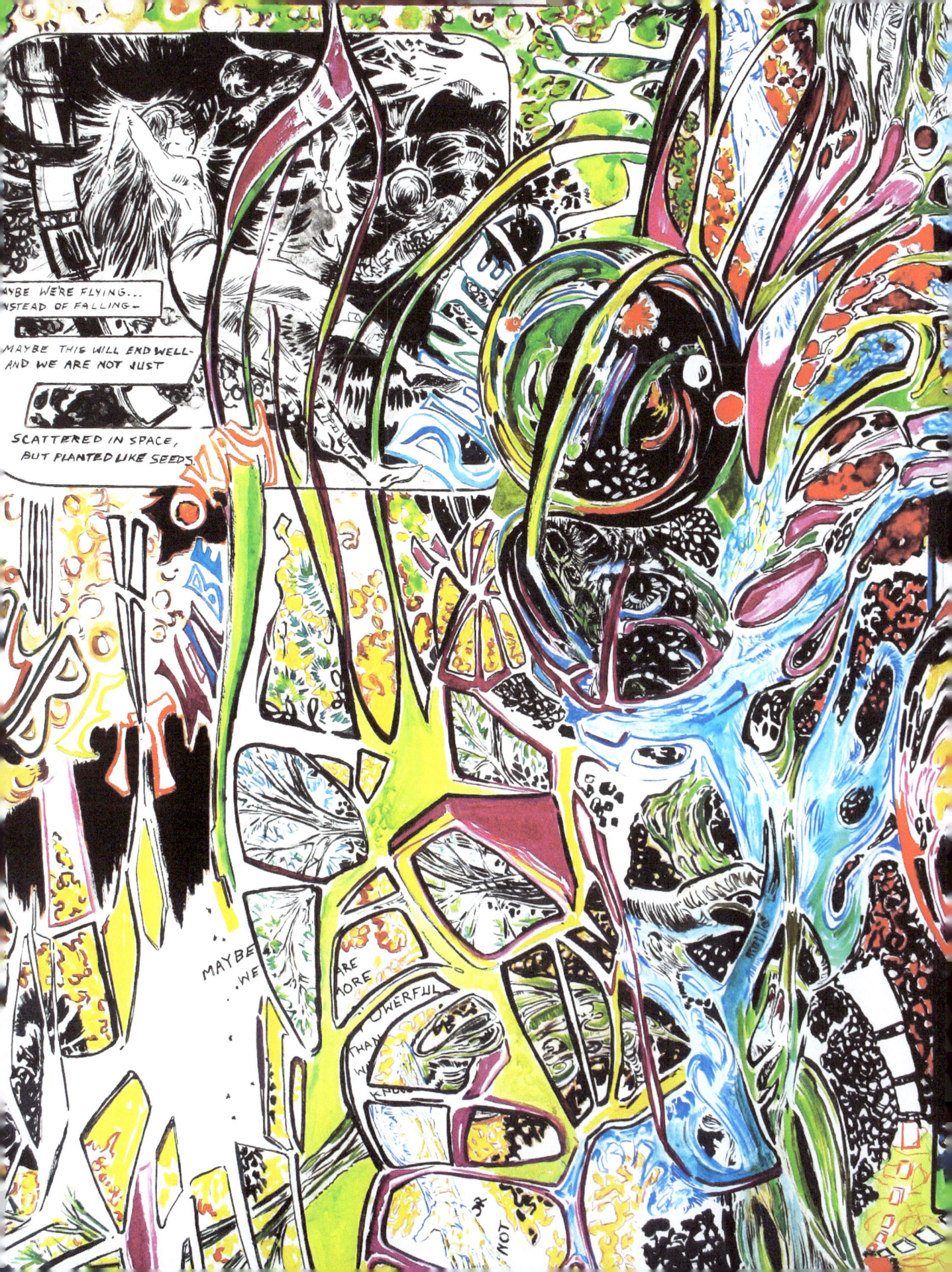

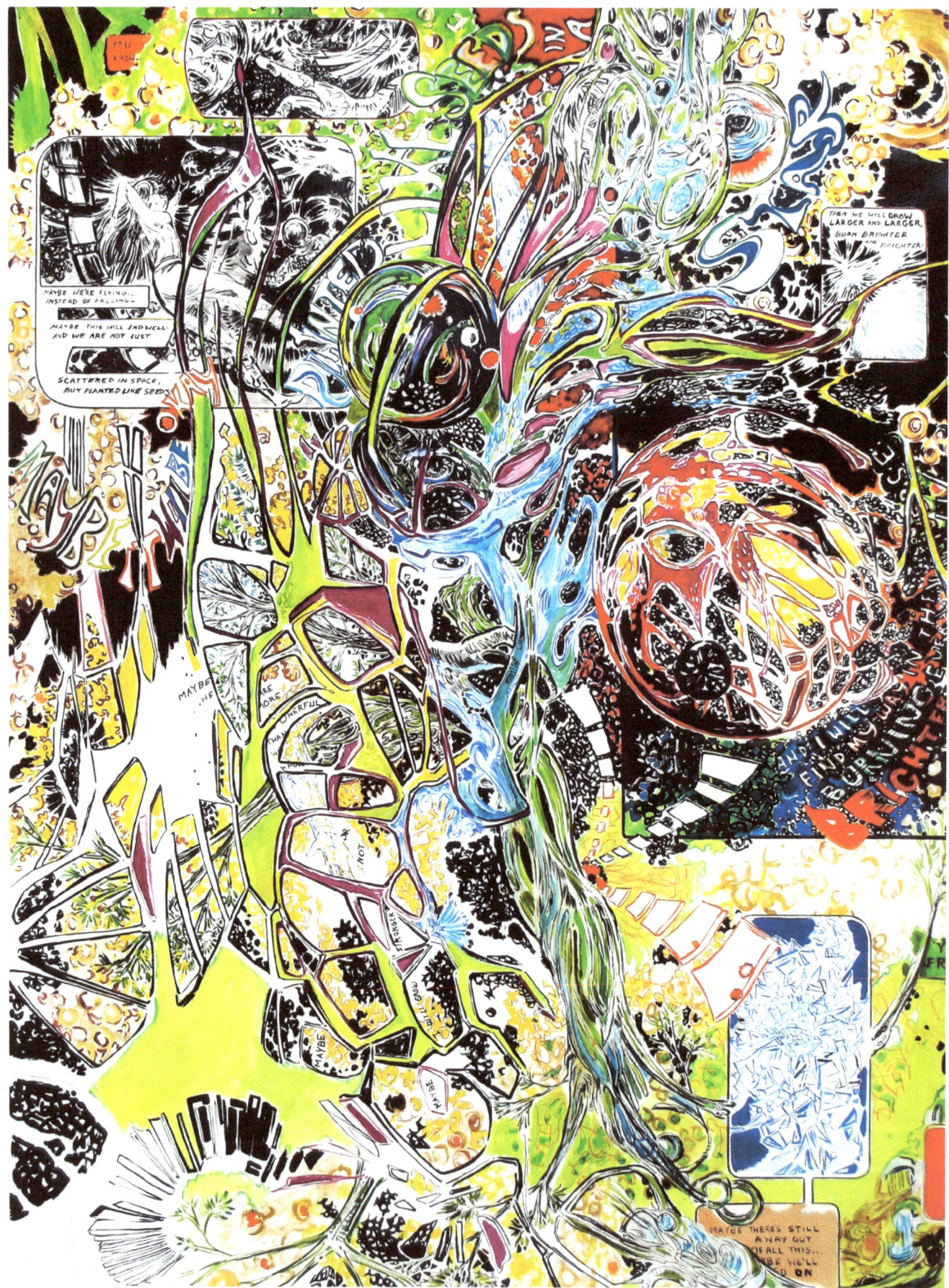

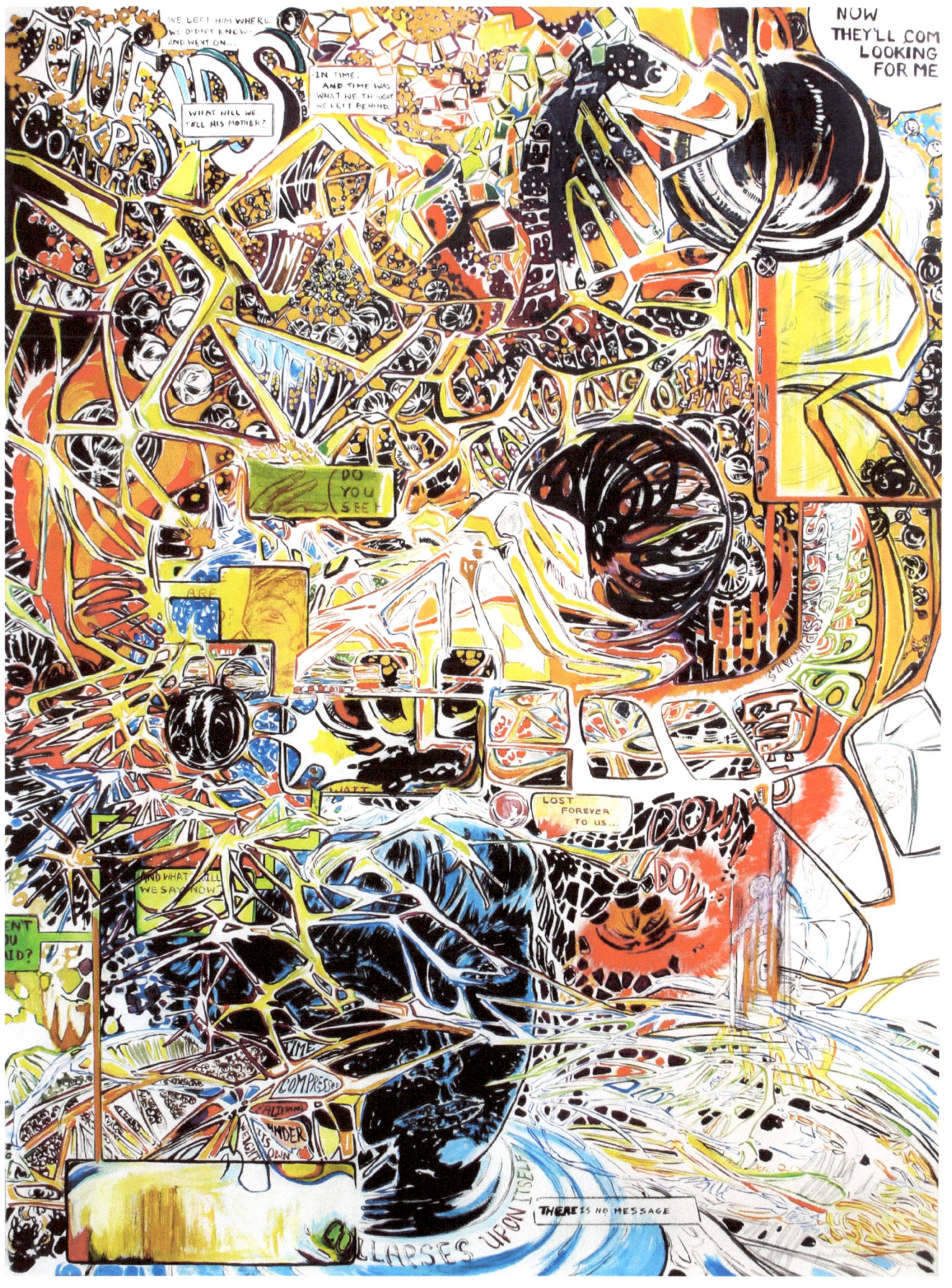

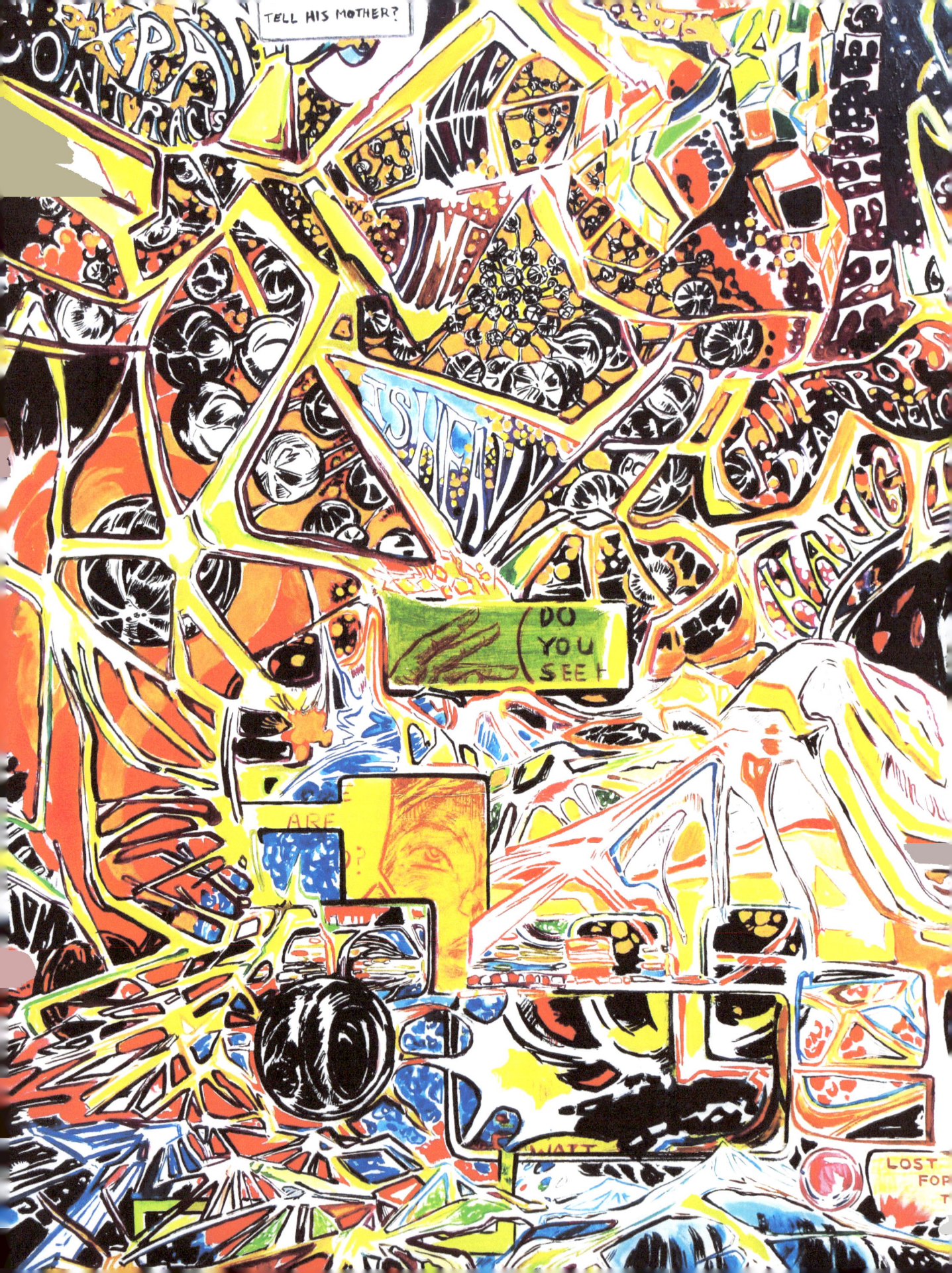

Universechild 12: time collapses upon itself (what will we tell his mother?)

(detail)

< overleaf: Universechild 12

Universechild

List of Works

Universechild 1, part 1: it took us much longer than we thought
Universechild 1, part 2: into the Universechild
Universechild 2: we could have anything we wanted and everything
we imagined would become real so we no longer wanted anything
Universechild 3: everything here is alive and everything is here
Universechild 4: we thought it would be wonderful
Universechild 5: eternity of empty space
Universechild 6: never shoot a gun in outer space
Universechild 7: no time
Universechild 8: everyone I know is somewhere else
Universechild 9: sometimes you know you are dreaming and you try
to change the dream into something better, something more perfect
Universechild 10: open and closed systems (will the city pay for this?)
Universechild 11: planted like seeds in a star
Universechild 12: time collapses upon itself (what will we tell his mother?)

all images 2003 – 2011, 36" x 48" or 48" x 36"
pencil, liquid acrylic, ink, colored pencil on paper

James Pustorino is an artist, curator and arts organizer in the NJ/NY metropolitan area. His work has been featured in exhibitions at the Butler Institute of American Art, the Columbus Museum of Art and in various public art projects.

NEW DRAWING presents series of innovative, current images from artists whose work explores and expands the visual and conceptual language of drawing.

Other books in the Series include:
Jill Scipione: Skullnotebook
Carl Vierow: Detective at Red Castle Pier and other Drawings

Victory Hall Press is a division of Victory Hall Inc., a not-for-profit arts organization producing exhibitions, events, education programs, public projects and publications, based in the NJ/NY metro area.

Visit our website at www.victoryhallpress.org

www.ingramcontent.com/pod-product-compliance
Lightning Source LLC
Chambersburg PA
CBHW051054180526
45172CB00002B/630